BLOOD, SWEAT & HONOR

MEMOIRS OF A "WALKING DEAD" MARINE IN VIETNAM

To Clint and Ashley our dear Christian friends and Church leaders,
Semper Fi

DERL HORN

Derl Horn
Phil 4:13

BLOOD, SWEAT AND HONOR
Memoirs of a "Walking Dead" Marine in Vietnam
Copyright © 2015 by Derl Horn
All rights reserved. No part of this book may be reproduced or transmitted in any form or by any means without written permission from the author.
ISBN 978-1511419451
Printed in USA by Createspace

DEDICATION

*I dedicate this book to my wife, Marilyn for her love,
support, and for praying me back home. Also to my children,
Cynthia Marshall, Cathy Denton and Chris Horn for the encouragement
they have given me to write and publish this book for our family. I also want to
dedicate this book to all my First Battalion, Ninth Marine Regiment, Third
Marine Division brothers and to the memory of my brothers who gave
their lives as the ultimate sacrifice for our country.*

TABLE OF CONTENTS

Chapter		
	Introduction	1
1	The Beginning	3
2	Boot Camp	9
3	Advance Training	19
4	Time with Family and First Assignment	21
5	Guantanamo Bay, Cuba	25
6	Vietnam Bound	31
7	Vietnam, The Reality	37
8	Ready for Action	43
9	Operation Cimarron in Quang Tri Province	49
10	Letters from Home	53
11	Con Thien, "The Hill of Angels"	55
12	Operation Buffalo	59
13	Ambush at the DMZ	63
14	Alarming Letter Home	89
15	Recuperate and Regroup	93
16	Operation Hickory II	97
17	Marilyn's Birthday	103
18	Back to Camp Carroll	105
19	Rest and Relaxation	109
20	Operation Kingfisher	113
21	Back to Con Thien	119
22	Killing Our Own	123
23	Marine Corps 199th Birthday	135
24	Our Wedding Anniversary	145
25	Twin Daughters!	149
26	Rock Ape Ambush	153
27	Letter from Lieutenant Colonel J. F. Mitchell	155
28	Rest and Relaxation in Hong Kong	157
29	Merry Christmas in Vietnam	165
30	Back to Hill 51	167
31	Back to Khe Sanh	171
32	Heading Home	177
33	Home with Family	183

ACKNOWLEDGMENTS

I want to thank my wife and best friend, Marilyn, for the many hours that she has given to editing my book as well as for writing her memories of events during those years. She encouraged me to continue writing along with our children, Cynthia Marshall, Cathy Denton, and Chris Horn.

I am deeply grateful to the Shiloh Writing Guild: Terry Siegler, Pam Long, Jan Hixson, Dr. Jeff Baker, Susan Wareford, Gwen Rockwood, and my grandson, Noah Marshall for their suggestions and editing help. Thanks to my editing friends, June Moore, Marilyn Fields, Herb and Jo Ray. A special thank you to my book editor Rene' A. Holt.

Thank you Jon Forst with Fringe Photo & Design for the exceptional design of my book cover and the editing of old photographs.

Thank you Denise Smith for your help with the layout of photographs in the book.

I appreciate all my relatives and friends who have supported me in writing *Blood, Sweat and Honor: Memoirs of a "Walking Dead" Marine in Vietnam* about my service in the United States Marine Corps, from 1966 through 1968.

Wedding Day, November 30, 1963

INTRODUCTION

Crack! Crack! The gooks fired their AK-47s all around the crater where we were huddled together. I realized that we had a very small chance of survival. Our options were few because we were so outnumbered and about to be overrun. We could stay where we were and be killed or captured and tortured; or we could run and take our chances. My decision was to run.

"Tom, I'm going to run. Give me cover." I requested. "When I get to safety, I will cover you." I prayed as I jumped from the crater, "Lord, please protect me and return me home to my family." I began to run, expecting cover from Hines, but as he fired his first shot, his rifle jammed from all the dirt.

With little protection from the gooks, I made my move. They were screaming and throwing grenades, making it difficult to stay on my feet. I could hear the bullets from their rifles landing with a thud around me, tearing up the ground as I ran a zigzag pattern as fast as I could. My only protection was the .45 pistol issued to me as the mortar gunner. I was running for my life, looking for cover and expecting at any moment to suffer the pain of the bullets. I was sprinting through a metal hail storm, but God truly placed His shield of protection around me.

The following pages tell of my journey through hell and back in the war of Vietnam, the most difficult and life-changing experiences I have ever known.

I was drafted into the Marines at twenty-three and trained to obey orders without question, defend myself, my fellow Marines and my country. I was called on to perform many things and assume a role contrary to my soft-hearted nature. My country had asked me to help defend a foreign nation crying out for their freedom, and I knew people would die.

July 2nd, 1967. Bravo Company's 2nd and 3rd Platoons were almost destroyed leaving only a few of their men along with our Mortar squad to battle the enemy. The NVA had done a good job of digging in with spider holes and trenches, along with snipers in the trees. They caught us in a U-shaped crossfire ambush with no place to go. We were hit with crisscrossing mortars, rockets and automatic weapons fire that killed fifty-nine of our Marines and wounded another sixty-five.

I believe I had a distinct advantage over most of my comrades because at the tender age of twelve, I had trusted the Lord Jesus Christ as my personal Savior and was determined to live my life for Him. I had no doubt He loved me and knew that He would be with me, even in the jungles of Vietnam. As I look back on those years of service in the Marines, I can clearly see how God guided and protected me as He deepened my faith and trust in Him daily.

This is my story...

1
THE BEGINNING

In February of 1966, my involvement with the Marine Corps and the Vietnam War began during a troubled time in our nation's history. It was a journey…a journey that was an unexpected adventure in my young life. This conflict had divided our country because many Americans felt we did not need to be involved. Although officially called a conflict by our government, it was a war for the soldiers, airmen, sailors, and Marines who fought. In the 1960s our country had instituted the draft for men eighteen years of age and older. At the time, many young men were concerned about being drafted and having their lives disrupted. Many of them felt the war was wrong and were able to get a deferment by attending a college or university. Others escaped the draft by leaving our country and living in Canada or Sweden. In the future they would be pardoned by the president.

As required in the United States, I registered with the draft board when I turned eighteen. After signing up with the draft board, I received two requests to take my physicals in Little Rock, Arkansas. I passed both times but was not drafted. I felt it was my duty to serve my country if called upon, but it didn't erase the fear I felt about going into a war zone and being separated from my wife, Marilyn Buchanan Horn. We had been married for two years, and our whole future lay before us.

Marilyn had been my high school sweetheart, but at that time we were having fun learning the roles of husband and wife. I had attended college at the University of Arkansas and was, at that time, selling life insurance. With my name on the draft list, waiting to receive a notice to report was nerve-racking. I had hoped being married might move my name down the list and give me more time at home. I was also thinking that, at twenty-three, I might be too old for the draft. With the prospect of being drafted heavy on my mind, I went by the draft office in Fayetteville, Arkansas several times to check where my name was on the list, but the draft board could not or would not tell me my position. The officer did say that my name was on the list and that I would be drafted at some point which made me anxious to know when the orders would come.

One day, when I felt I could wait no longer, I went down to the draft board and told them to move my name to the top of the list. I could not endure the waiting any longer. They again refused to comply and told me to go home and check my mailbox. I hurried home to our garage apartment and checked my mail. I found the dreaded draft papers. The letter read: "Greetings, You are hereby ordered for induction into the Armed Forces of the United States, and to report at National Guard Armory-10 South College-Fayetteville, Arkansas on February 24, 1966 at 9:00 a.m. for forwarding to an Armed Forces Induction Station."

Since I had passed the physical twice already, I felt certain I was headed for a tour of duty in the United States Army. Finally I was relieved of the pressure of waiting and not knowing where I was going, but I was very sad to leave Marilyn and all our plans for the future.

On February 24, 1966, I boarded a Greyhound bus from Fayetteville for travel to Little Rock to take my physical with several other draftees and volunteers who, for the most part, were young men fresh out of high school. Our bus driver dropped us off at the YMCA in Little Rock where we spent the night. The next morning we were transferred downtown to the recruiting area where we were put through physical and mental testing. At the conclusion, fifty of us waited to be assigned for training. I assumed that I would go to an Army base close to home for my training, possibly Camp Polk in Louisiana or Fort Chaffee in Arkansas. I hoped that Marilyn could visit me on the weekends, but I quickly realized that was not going to happen.

As I waited with the group of young men for our assignments at the Armed Forces Examining and Entrance Station, the door opened and in walked four Marine Corps officers. They informed those in charge that they needed five Marine recruits. They were then given permission to take their pick. Trying to hide, I avoided eye contact with the officers, hoping they would not choose me. Just as I looked away, one of them pointed to me and said, "We want that one." He then went on to select James R. Smith from Broken Arrow, Oklahoma, Kenneth E. Boyd from Fayetteville, Arkansas, and two men from Springdale, Arkansas, Thomas A. Johnston and Donald E. Clark. I spoke up and said, "I did not come here to join the Marine Corps and would prefer just to go on into the Army." The officer told me that I could make that choice, but I would have to serve a year longer in the Army. I responded, "I guess you have yourself a Marine."

The Vietnam War was only the second time in the history of the Marine Corps to use the draft; the first time was World War II. I was one of the few chosen and in a few months, I would become a Marine. I wondered how they made their decisions in selecting "a few good men." I soon learned how tough the drill instructors (DIs) would be on an older, married man who had not volunteered but was drafted.

By 4:00 p.m. I had signed the necessary papers and had my orders in hand. I found a phone and sadly informed my wife of what had taken place and where I was headed. I started out by saying, "Honey, I will be going to San Diego, California for my training." She immediately knew what that meant. Her brother, Kenneth Buchanan, who was a senior in high school, had already signed up with the Marine Corps and was gung ho to start his training. Marilyn said, "Oh no! Why did you join the Marines?" and began to cry. Her brother heard her say Marines in the background and began to jump and shout, "Derl is going to be a Marine!" He was overjoyed about it. Marilyn was devastated as I tried to explain the situation to her, but at that point, she was too distraught to understand. Her brother was shouting with joy while she sobbed, heartbroken and disappointed. That was our last conversation for four long weeks.

Marilyn: I could not believe my ears as Derl shared that he was going to San Diego. I knew it was the Marine training center. I was heartbroken and could not stop crying, knowing we would be separated for several months. Gone in an instant was my hope of joining him after his initial training. The phone conversation was brief, leaving me with more questions than answers. Little did I realize at that moment it would be several more weeks before I would hear his voice again. All I could do was pray, be patient, and wait.

There are two locations where men are trained to become Marines: the Recruit Training Depot at Parris Island, South Carolina and the Recruit Training Depot at San Diego, California. I was assigned to San Diego because I lived west of the Mississippi in the small town of Springdale, Arkansas. San Diego graduates more than twenty-one thousand Marines per year; Parris Island graduates more than seventeen thousand per year.

Marine Corps boot camp is more challenging, both physically and mentally, than the basic training programs of the other military branches of service. Not only are the physical requirements much higher, but recruits are required to learn and memorize a huge amount of information. The training period is a little longer than twelve weeks. We studied the history of the Marine Corps in depth. We were required to memorize the eleven General Orders for a Sentry, the Rifle Creed, "The Marine Corps Hymn," the USMC Core Values, the Code of Conduct, and the characteristics of the M14 rifle. I trained in basic training with the M14 rifle. In my Infantry Training Regiment (ITR), I trained with the M1 rifle and later fought in Vietnam with the M16 rifle.

Recruit Training Depot - San Diego, California

Platoon 358, Derl on 3rd row, 6th from left

Derl Horn - Marine Corps Recruit Depot

2
BOOT CAMP

On February 25, 1966, at 5:12 p.m., I was on my way to San Diego with four other recruits. We all tried to enjoy our plane ride; the steak dinners served on Delta Airlines from Little Rock to Dallas and from Dallas to San Diego made it more enjoyable. That was the day we later longed for as we dreamed of good meals on a flight headed back home. After landing in San Diego at 9:06 p.m., two Marine Corps representatives greeted us at the airport. They were nice and courteous as they escorted us to a bus and we all found seats on the bus. But as the bus door slammed shut, the world as we knew it was left behind. The "nice" Marines screamed at us, calling us names we had never been called before, such as *maggots, scumbags, girls, ladies*, and all kinds of profane names. They informed us that we were to sit at attention and not look to the left or right but silently straight ahead. This command was difficult because as we passed through San Diego for the first time, we were curious and wanted to look around. I was scared and thought, *Lord, what have I done?*

When we arrived around 9:30 p.m. at the Marine Corps Recruit Depot (MCRD) in San Diego, we were herded off the bus and told to stand on the footsteps painted red on the pavement. The DIs screamed at us to stay on the footsteps and to stand at attention. We were like a herd of cattle with no idea how to stand at attention or anything else, for that matter

We were put in line for haircuts and asked, "How would you like your hair cut?" After telling them, they completely shaved our heads.

They remained that way for the entire sixteen weeks of basic and initial training. The haircut became a weekly ritual.

Following the haircut, we were marched over to Recruit Receiving to get our gear: combat boots and uniforms that we would use throughout basic training. I felt that I looked like Gomer Pyle because almost everything issued to me was either too big or too small. As the clothes and boots were literally thrown at me, the Marines called me "fatso." I struggled to control my temper. Back home I had been an insurance salesman for over a year and had gained a few pounds. I weighed 142 pounds for most of my adult life, but now my weight had crept up to 160. I was almost six feet tall, yet they were calling me fat! The on-duty Marine placed all of our civilian clothes and other belongings in a box to be shipped home, stripping us of everything that reminded us of home. I was assigned to Platoon 358 along with eighty-eight other men who made up the platoon.

After receiving the clothing, we were assigned to our Quonset huts and bunk beds, with approximately twenty recruits per hut. I was glad to get a bottom bunk. At 2:30 a.m., we crawled into bed. I lay there wondering how I could survive this kind of treatment. Drifting off to sleep, I dreamed of Marilyn and how happy she had made me during our first two years and three months of marriage.

I woke up long after daylight with the sun shining in. I was so surprised that it was already 0900 hours (9:00 a.m.). I thought, *This might not be too bad if we are allowed to sleep in.* That was the first and last time we slept late for the rest of training. From that day on, we were abruptly awakened before daylight with reveille and the DIs screaming obscenities while rushing us to the showers, breakfast, and training.

Our drill instructors, GySgt. W. R. Hunt, SSgt. J. Wilkinson, Sgt. G. W. Harty, and Sgt. G. F. Moylan, had a difficult job ahead, but they worked hard week after week to transform us from a group of slouching civilians into a company of men who stood straight, tall, and proud. We would feel pride in what we had accomplished and how we had changed. During our training time at MCRD we were treated like prisoners.

The DI's gave us instructions about head (bathroom) duties, and all general information about our training, as well as where and how to eat, sleep, and shower. They shared with us the best spot to go AWOL (absent without leave). If we felt we couldn't hack it, they explained how to commit suicide by slicing our wrist the proper way. They did not want us to do a partial job, they wanted us to make it final. I was thinking, *these DI's are truly nuts.*

DI, Sgt. Moylan loved the actor John Wayne. Every night after he gave the order to hit the rack (bed) he made us say, "Good night, John Wayne." After we were in the racks he would call us to attention, telling us that we had better be at attention when he returned the next morning or there would be "hell to pay." Thankfully, each morning one of the recruits would hear him coming toward the hut and give a warning to the rest of us. We would all be lying at attention in our racks when he came storming in.

The mess hall food was good and there was plenty of it. Our first morning, we were marched into the mess hall for breakfast and informed by our DI to take all the food we wanted but we were to clean our plate. The first thing I saw was a table with all kinds of fruit on it so I took a banana, an apple and an orange. As we moved down the chow line, the "on-duty" recruit piled large amounts of food on our trays. It was enough for three meals. We were so full that it hurt for us to do the physical exercises, the running and the drills. At the time, none of us knew that we could have refused to take certain food items; we thought we were required to eat everything offered to us.

One morning I said, "Yes sir," to one of the recruits putting food on my tray and he said, "Don't yes sir me!" I am only a recruit just like you, and you don't have to take everything that is offered." I thanked him, relieved to know we would not have to eat such large amounts of food at each meal. We learned the tray procedure was to side step down the chow line at attention, holding our tray forward for food and pulling it back to refuse an item. During my required week of mess duty, I felt compassion for the new recruits and shared with them the food and tray policy.

The week of mess duty was a tough week of manual labor. We were up early to prepare and serve the chow three times a day and then after the meals, we also worked as the cleanup crew. It did not take long to fall into our racks at night completely exhausted after a 16-hour day.

The rifle drills and marching on the grinder (parade ground) was difficult at first. As recruits, we were punished each time anybody made a wrong move, and it seemed we were always making mistakes.

The punishment was either doing a hundred push-ups or running for hours or holding our rifle across the backside of our finger tips until our backs felt like they were breaking. Learning to clean our rifles was important so we would have clean, working rifles that would pass inspection. If we failed, we learned another discipline called "funerals for our rifles." This event happened when the DI would inspect our rifles and declare them as either clean or dirty. If they were not clean, we would have to dig a 6-ft x 2-ft hole to bury our rifles in. After the burial, we would dig up the rifle and clean it again for another inspection. If it failed the second inspection, there was another "funeral." It felt endless, and pointless. I wondered if our rifles would ever be clean.

Most recruits were smokers so there were specific rules for them. We had to wait until the DI informed us that "the smoking lamp was lit" but you could not light up a cigarette until he said, "Light 'em up." If you lit before he gave the word, you would have to smoke the whole cigarette with a 2-gallon bucket placed over your head while your hands remained in your pockets. This punishment would cause us to cough and choke as we tried to breathe. If we didn't receive the bucket punishment, the DI would assign us to some other dirty work detail. We were allowed to have one or two cigarette a day if the DI was in a good mood. The DI informed us when "the smoking lamp was out." It was then that the cigarette butt had to be field stripped which consisted of tearing the leftover part of the cigarette open and spreading the tobacco and the rolled up paper on the ground. The paper and tobacco were biodegradable so they weren't considered "litter." If we forgot to field strip the cigarette butt, we would have to dig a 3-foot x 3-foot hole and bury it. As soon as we finished burying the butt, the DI would want to see what brand it was so we would dig it up to show him and then bury it again. Sometimes the DI would say, "The smoking lamp is lit for one cigarette" and then he would say, "And I will smoke it." At that time he would smoke and make the recruits watch.

Letter writing was usually allowed on Sunday afternoons. All the men would sit on the buckets we used for various cleaning jobs. We would write with paper on our laps as the DI's walked around looking over our shoulder to read what we were writing. My first letter home to Marilyn was written with the DI standing over me, dictating what to write to her. He would say things like, "Tell her that your DI's are nice and that you like it here." I felt bad writing those lies to her because I did not like all the control and felt much dislike for my DI's. They controlled every word we said and every move we made. I know now that it was all in the training, but hard to accept at that time.

Marilyn – Letters were our lifeline and each one was a treasure that I read over and over. Daily I wrote Derl giving him the news from home along with all my questions, checking to see how he was adjusting, asking about the food and training and if he was making friends. His letters were short and did not come near often enough. I was doing my best to adjust to the separation but it was challenging. After being married for two years and enjoying my independence it was difficult to move back home with my parents and brothers. I was very homesick for Derl, and everywhere I went there were reminders of the fun we had had together, at home, at church and in the community. I continued in my job with the Shakespeare Company assembling fishing reels, hoping that staying busy would help me fill up the long hours, making the weeks pass quickly.

After that experience, I wrote my letters with a penlight under my blanket after lights were out. I cannot imagine what would have happened if I had been caught, but I loved my wife dearly and wanted her to know the truth of what I was experiencing. I sneaked them into the envelopes during our letter writing times on Sunday.

After the first week, letters started arriving from home. Some letters smelled good with perfume, and others had SWAK (sealed with a kiss) on the envelope or lipstick kisses. Any Marine that received letters of this nature had to open and read them out loud to the rest of us, and sometimes the DI would just smell the envelope, announce who it was for and discard it. I wrote Marilyn and told her not to put anything special on the envelope or I would experience all kinds of harassment. One recruit received a two pound box of fudge. The DI made him sit on his bucket and eat it all in front of us and of course, it made him very sick.

Telephone calls home were rare. We were only allowed to call home twice during our twelve weeks of basic training. During our initial four weeks of specialized training, we got permission to call home on weekends. We all looked forward to making those phone calls. However, we still had to wait in line for a phone while having another impatient recruit standing behind us, anxiously waiting so he could make his call. There was no privacy.

Marilyn- Finally after four weeks the phone rang, it was Derl, I was so excited to hear his voice as it felt like it had been years instead of weeks since we last talked. He immediately explained that our visit would be short because of a long line of men waiting to make their calls. Feeling the pressure of having only a few minutes to talk caused us to hurriedly begin sharing information and asking questions. Derl reassured me that he was fine, the training was difficult but he was surviving. We were both near tears because we were extremely homesick, but we ended our conversation by encouraging each other with the reminder that God would guide us through our separation. As we said our good-byes we expressed our love to each other but it was hard to hang up the phone not knowing when I would hear his voice again.

The DI's seem to delight in harassing and embarrassing us in front of the other recruits. The main harassment I received was about my age. I was twenty three years old, older than most recruits, married and was drafted into the Marine Corps. The DI's would say, "This is a volunteer Marine Corps so what is a draftee doing here?" The other thing I often heard was, "If we wanted you to have a wife, we would have issued you one." This caused me to be really angry but I realized that to react would give them reason for more harassment and extra duties.

Payday was another dreaded day, because the DI's had us parade through their hut at attention as they passed out our pay. They always singled me out and shamed me for being married and sending an allotment home. I almost had to beg for my money, to the point that I was afraid that I would not get it. I can laugh about it now but at the time it was not funny.

Our DI's had a rule that we could not go to the head until 30 minutes had passed after taps had been played. Taps is a twenty four note bugle call that is a signal for "lights out" and "all is well" at the end of a serviceman's day. Taps is also used for the final call at military funerals. Reveille is a military bugle call played at dawn to awaken the troops for morning roll call and the posting of the National Colors. After thirty minutes of waiting for "lights out," I would be so tired that I would fall asleep without a visit to the head. The next morning, I would be miserable again since I had to wait another thirty minutes before going to the head. Out of desperation there were times I secretly used my bucket to relieve myself. Thank God I was never caught. The head was crowded each morning with the whole platoon trying to prepare for the day. We never had enough time. The DI's were constantly screaming at us to hurry and get finished.

One poor recruit wet his bed several times but managed to cover up the evidence temporarily. After the platoon flunked a bunk inspection, he was caught. The DI went on an angry rampage, stripping all our beds and dumping all our trunks containing everything we had onto the floor in one heap. The DI's found the wet sheets. They were brutal to this man as they screamed and yelled at him. They ended their fury by giving him double foot kicks in the stomach that sent him tumbling head over heels. Eventually he landed in the sick bay (hospital). While he was gone, the DI's explained to the platoon what was to be done to this man when he returned. He was to experience a "blanket party." This prank was done when someone holds the platoon back, causes trouble, or is disliked by the DI. During the "blanket party," the recruits in the platoon were to throw a blanket over the "trouble maker" during the night, and then all the recruits would beat him up. After this man's return from the sick bay and after the "blanket party" beating, this poor guy never wet the bed again, but he did have to spend more time in the sick bay. I felt sorry for the "blanket party" recruit because he was in so much pain. I have a soft heart so I would pretend to hit him, but would never land a punch. If the DI realized that I did not participate in the beating, I would have been the next blanket party victim.

As a platoon we learned many skills during our Boot Camp training. We learned how to be disciplined: how to march, to dress, to spit shine boots, to polish our brass, to starch our covers (utility caps), to run, to fall, to carry a wounded comrade, to throw a grenade, to shoot properly, to perform hand to hand combat, to use our bayonet, to crawl under wire fences while machine guns were fired over head, to survive in water, to shoot many different weapons, to survive gas attacks, to react automatically to any given situation, and to function as a team. We were being trained to kill the enemy and to survive.

Each platoon member learned to use the pugil stick, a heavily padded pole-like training weapon, used to train for rifle and bayonet combat. During one pugil stick fight, I was in control of my opponent and happy that it was going well when I felt a painful attack from the rear knocking me to my knees. The DI had seen my success and added another recruit into the ring, giving me two opponents for a double beating. In war nothing is fair, and neither is it in training.

The gas mask training was something I will never forget. We were marched to an insulated shed out from the main base area. The whole platoon was herded into the shed and told to put on our gas masks. The DI turned on the tear gas and then made us take off our masks and sing the Marine Corps hymn all the way through before we could put our masks back on. That was a sight to see. The smell of the gas and the stinging of our eyes made for a bunch of slobbering, blubbering Marines.

Rifle qualifying day was on the rifle range with our M14 rifles. During this time, we would march to the rifle range before daylight and wait for the sun to come up. On some days with the fog rolling in, we would have to wait until noon before we could see the targets.

The DI would yell "Ready on the right, ready on the left, begin firing." I was a good shot on the rifle range. On the first day of practice, I qualified as an Expert. However on the official qualifying day I qualified one step down as a Sharpshooter. Later I would thank God for this lower qualification as I realized it most likely kept me from being assigned as a sniper. It is one thing to kill, but a sniper sees through his telescope what happens as the bullet enters the body.

We had some recruits who did not qualify during the week and that was considered a disgrace. One young recruit next to me struggled to hit the target, so the DI grabbed his hand and bit his trigger finger, making it sore and sensitive. The injury caused him to pull the trigger gently allowing him to hit the targets and qualify. Other times the DI's would prick the recruit's fingers with pins to make them sensitive so that the recruit pulled the trigger lightly and would not jerk and miss the target. It seemed the DI's wanted the recruits to succeed and was offering their help through this crude training method. Any time a recruit missed the target, recruits at the target pit would wave "Maggie's drawers" (a flag with a red disc to let him know that he missed the target). The recruits took turns shooting and working in the target pits.

DERL HORN

At last graduation day arrived. We had finished our basic training and were ready for graduation. What a wonderful experience to graduate from boot camp and to be called a true Marine! Now our DI's talked to us in a different manner. They treated us with respect, calling us Marines instead of the usual scumbags and other profane names they had used for the last twelve weeks.

Graduation was an exciting day and I felt a sense of accomplishment and pride, as we marched onto the parade deck in front of all the dignitaries with the band playing The Marine Corps Hymn, with family and friends waving from the stands. My family lived too far away to attend my graduation, but I was happy and relieved to know I was finished with boot camp.

After the graduation ceremony, as we were being bused out of the basic training area and headed for our advance training, I saw a recruit who had started out with our platoon. He had been very overweight and out of shape. When we arrived he could not do a single sit up, pull up or push up, so he was removed from our platoon and placed in a physical training platoon, otherwise known as the "fat farm." There the recruit exercised and ran all day and was given a very restricted diet until he was able to go through the basic training. As I looked back, I realized he was still running and had not even started his Basic Training. He appeared to have lost a lot of weight and looked much better. I felt sorry for him, but I was happy to be leaving.

Infantry Training Regiment - Camp Pendleton, CA

Richard Glass and Derl during training

Derl with M14 at ITR

3
ADVANCE TRAINING

My next phase was Infantry Training Regiment (ITR) at Camp Pendleton. We were now treated as Marines. We no longer had a DI, but we did have troop handlers and trainers. The intense training required us to think and plan more on our own and as a team. The majority of us were being trained for Vietnam. The troop handlers and trainers were Vietnam and Korean War veterans. No matter what field they assigned us to, the Marine Corps tradition was to train each and every man to be a fighting Marine, able to kill the enemy.

Our training focused on company, platoon, squad and fire team tactics and deployment in patrolling, ambush, attack, and defense. Other areas of training included infiltration under live fire; field craft; camouflage; the latest infantry weapons; use of military explosives, grenades, and flame-throwers; mine warfare identification; and night tactics.

We were issued the M1 carbine rifle. The Browning automatic rifle (BAR) was used as the fire team support weapon. Other weapons were the M-79 grenade launcher, M-14 rifle, .45 pistol, M-60 machine gun, 3.5 rocket launcher, 60mm and 81mm mortars. My Military Occupational Specialty (MOS) was the 81mm mortar. Weighing 136 pounds, the 81mm mortar breaks down into four sections and is carried by four men. The rate of fire is eighteen rounds per minute and the maximum range is 3,290 yards.

I was assigned to a fire team with Mike Hogan, Bill Holmes, and

Tim Haley. Three of the men were from California; however, as the "Old Arkie" from Arkansas, I was the exception. Since Hogan was our team leader, we soon were labeled "Hogan's Heroes" after the TV series. We were a good team and worked well together.

The ITR training lasted approximately five weeks. We were then given our orders for our next assignment. I was assigned to Camp Lejuene, North Carolina, for more specialized training with the 81mm mortar and in warfare tactics.

4

TIME WITH FAMILY AND FIRST ASSIGNMENT

    Finally, I was on leave and headed home to see my beautiful wife, Marilyn, and my family. Military service personnel were allowed to fly free on standby, or they could pay their own fare for a regular ticket. Since money was scarce, most recruits flew home on standby. The trip seemed to take forever, but my flight finally landed at the Tulsa International Airport. I was thrilled to see Marilyn again after being separated for seventeen long weeks. The moment our eyes met, we couldn't get to each other fast enough for a long hug and many kisses. We were so thankful to be together again. We loaded up my sea bag in our little Chevy II and headed to dinner and a hotel in Tulsa. We enjoyed resting, relaxing, and catching up on all we had missed during my training. A few days later we headed home to Springdale to visit family and friends. Words could not describe how happy we were to be together.

    One funny incident happened while on leave when my brother-in-law Kenneth invited me to join him for target practice. We drove to a hillside not far from home where it would be safe to shoot. Kenneth proceeded to set up wooden matches fifty yards away as my target. He was anxious to see my shooting skills, knowing I had qualified as a sharpshooter during training. I took aim with the 22-caliber rifle and shot, striking the match head and igniting it. I was shocked, but Kenneth was not surprised; he had expected me to hit the target. It was just luck, but in Kenneth's eyes I was a true Marine. Being admired by Kenneth gave me pure Marine pride.

After enjoying a short visit with family and friends, Marilyn and I loaded the car to begin our trip to Camp Lejeune for my next assignment. It was June 1966, a very hot summer with record high temperatures across the nation, making the trip a miserable drive in a car without air-conditioning. We had packed an ice chest with water and a cloth to wipe our faces to help keep us cool. The car was loaded down with all the stuff we needed for our apartment. Looking back, I'm surprised we didn't break a spring or blow a tire because the car was so overloaded. We enjoyed the beautiful drive across Tennessee and North Carolina, seeing the countryside, and stopping along the way at tourist spots. This trip was a big one for us since neither of us had ever traveled far from home.

Camp Lejeune Marine Corps Base is located on North Carolina's central coast, a beautiful part of our country. It lies directly south of Jacksonville and is divided into two parts by the New River. We enjoyed seeing the Atlantic Ocean for the first time. We stopped to walk on the warm sand and wade out into the ocean. We enjoyed listening to the waves and watching them crash into the beach. Arriving in Jacksonville in the early afternoon, we found a small air-conditioned motel close to a Howard Johnson's Motel. We could not afford to stay at the Howard Johnson's, but we enjoyed eating the many flavors of ice cream offered there. The small motel where we stayed had several things we were not expecting, like cockroaches—too many to count. We were told that these pests are a problem near coastal areas, but we were not interested in staying and dealing with them. Marilyn was terrified during that one-night stay and worked at keeping her feet up off the floor. Neither of us slept well, thinking we might end up sleeping with the cockroaches.

I reported for duty at the base the next morning and was informed that I would be going on a week of training for amphibious landing and field-training missions. My first few days at Camp Lejeune were spent playing war games, climbing off ships, and learning how to make beach landings.

This assignment made it urgent for us to find a place to live before I left. After seeing too many rundown and nasty apartments, we finally found a new apartment complex, housing mostly Marine families, in a beautiful wooded area with an abundance of pine trees. After paying a deposit for the apartment, we unloaded our car and began to unpack.

Marilyn dreaded having me leave her in an unfamiliar city for a week, not knowing a single soul. In a few days she became acquainted with some of the wives in the nearby apartments who also had husbands deployed or in field training. Some of our first friends were our next-door neighbors, Ken and Rosaline Morris. Ken was also a Marine. We enjoyed playing cards and having meals together. Ken was our alarm clock. Each morning he woke us with his loud, blood-curdling bear roar, announcing that he was awake. So was everyone else.

One Sunday afternoon, as we were playing cards with Ken and Rosaline in our apartment, we all smelled smoke. We jumped up to investigate and found the smoke coming from Ken and Rosaline's apartment. The smoke bellowed out from around their door, so we called the fire department. The firemen were delayed in arriving, and I felt we needed to take action immediately because of the danger to the adjoining apartments. Not thinking about any danger to myself, I opened the door and entered the smoky apartment. Rosaline had forgotten about a pan of grease she left on the stove. The grease caught fire in the skillet, then jumped and climbed up the wall. I grabbed a plastic container, filled it with water, and put out the fire. The firemen arrived, checked the apartment for damage and made sure the other apartments were safe before they left. Rosaline felt embarrassed but grateful to me for putting out the fire. It was an exciting afternoon.

Training at Camp Lejeune, NC

Firing 81mm mortar

Marilyn and Derl on USS North Carolina

Derl and Marine, Richard Glass

5

GUANTANAMO BAY, CUBA

After my return from the week of field training, I began extensive mortar training. I was now known as an official "brown bagger," meaning I lived off the base and carried my lunch each day.

The next few weeks were spent in classroom training and on field exercises, using the 81mm mortar. Six weeks into our stay at Camp Lejeune, I received orders for Guantanamo Bay, Cuba, called "GITMO" by most Marines. Disappointed about another separation, I now had to find a way to return Marilyn to her family. Her brother Tommy volunteered to ride a bus to Jacksonville and drive her back to Arkansas. He arrived a few days early to visit the base and to attend classes with me. Much of the classroom training was held outside under shade trees. Tommy must have been impressed with the Marines he met because, when he returned home, he enlisted. Now the Buchanan family would have their son-in-law, as well as both sons, in the Marine Corps, all at the same time. It was an unsettling time for the family as everyone realized that all three of us could end up fighting in Vietnam. I was grateful for the many hours of prayer the family offered for each of us.

Marilyn and I had another tearful good-bye, knowing that we would be apart for five months instead of the usual four months for this deployment. I realized that separations were difficult on a marriage because of the stress; a marriage could be strengthened or weakened by the separation. I was thankful that our marriage relationship grew stronger during this experience. We had an enduring love for each other that called us to be faithful to one another and to God. We both had received Christ as our Savior as young children, and we had committed our lives to following God and His Word.

Marilyn: *My brother and I headed back home on September 1, 1966. It was a long two-day trip without Derl, and I had lots of time to think about the hundreds of miles we were putting between us. After being separated during his two months of training, I had no illusions about how difficult the separation would be. The empty feeling of being apart and the sadness was overwhelming. All I wanted to do was cry. I had hours to think about the last two months we had enjoyed together at Camp Lejeune, making new friends, finding a new church, and exploring the Jacksonville area. It was hard to believe we only had two short months together before this deployment and now I was headed back home. My brother Tommy was driving and doing his best to make the trip fun. I was grateful he had been willing to ride the bus out and drive me back to Arkansas. We enjoyed visiting and seeing new parts of the country. He shared with me that he was seriously considering joining the Marine Corps. That news was upsetting, and I was trying hard to understand his desire to serve our country, especially during the awful Vietnam War, but he felt as an American, he should serve as did our dad and now Derl.*

September 2, 1966. Those deployed to Cuba packed up and boarded trucks for a convoy to the ocean to catch our ship, the troop carrier *USS Telafare*. I stood on the deck with Richard Glass and Dan Hoel. We watched the U.S. mainland grow smaller as the ship headed out to sea.

Our sleeping quarters were so close together that there was no way for me to sleep or even tolerate being in the cramped sleeping area. I took my blanket and slept on the deck which was allowed due to the crowded conditions. It was damp, but better than sleeping with my nose touching the person above me.

On the troop carrier, I experienced my first Navy shower. The shower procedure was to step into the shower stall, turn on the water, wet your body, turn off the water, soap down, turn the water back on, and rinse off. Then you were finished. It wasn't the greatest shower, but it was better than what I later experienced in Vietnam.

We traveled three days from the United States to Cuba. Every day we watched dolphins swimming alongside the ship, giving us a diversion and a bit of entertainment. The most enjoyable part of the trip for me was the opportunity to attend church services. The chaplain led the service, taught Bible classes, and directed the men in singing hymns together. All of this brought back feelings of home and made me miss being in church with Marilyn.

Our barracks at GITMO were chicken-house style buildings, long and open. The group showers were detached from our barracks. I was fortunate to have good friends with me, especially Richard Glass from Galveston, Texas. Friends since basic training, he and I would continue to run into each other during most of my tour.

While at Guantanamo Bay, our hot, humid, and boring job was rotating guard duty to keep the Cubans on their side of the fence. When not assigned to guard duty, we practiced drills at the base camp. Three days at a time, we would be out in the field to set up our 81mm mortars and stand guard.

At bedtime we were provided cots with mosquito nets, but the mosquitoes were big and plentiful, making it difficult to sleep. Each morning we had contests to see who had received the most bites. One day I counted twenty-one bites on my left hand. We sprayed mosquito repellent on our bodies at night, but they seemed to like it. We applied gun oil to our bites thinking that might help. Bunkers were available for sleeping, but the heat inside them was unbearable, so most men slept outside on cots or on the ground.

We never fired on the enemy because the Cuban military gunned down their own men as they tried to escape. If a deserter managed to avoid being shot, he could not survive the land mines covering both sides of the fence. During the night we heard gunfire or explosions and knew that one more Cuban had failed to escape.

While I was in Cuba, I had only one opportunity to call Marilyn by shortwave radio. We could not hear each other, but the radioman relayed our messages back and forth. It was a pathetic phone call but at least we talked to each other in real time. Our letters continued to be our lifeline as we wrote almost daily. Mail call was the highlight of each day, and I looked forward to those letters filled with loving, encouraging words.

Marilyn: *The holidays were upon us, and I was experiencing my first Thanksgiving and Christmas without Derl. The joyful season just seemed to intensify my loneliness. Listening to my favorite Christmas albums made me sad.*

I busied myself with making Christmas gifts—stockings for Derl and all our nieces and nephews. I helped mother decorate the house by putting up the tree, making different kinds of candy, and baking for our family dinners. This helped make the days pass quickly. I was anxious to turn the calendar and welcome in the new year of 1967, knowing that Derl would be coming home in the middle of January.

At the end of my tour in Cuba, we were shipped back to Camp Lejuene on the *USS Sandavar*, another crowded troop carrier. I didn't care. I was just glad to be headed back to the States. The trip was uneventful apart from the dolphins cruising alongside the ship and some Marines getting motion sickness. Again I slept topside on the damp and dirty deck to prevent seasickness. Upon my arrival back in the States, I telephoned Marilyn to let her know I was back at Camp Lejeune and would soon be coming to pick her up.

Derl second from the left

Guantanamo Bay, Cuba

Derl with 81mm mortar

"Junk on the bunk"

Leaving for Vietnam

Derl & brother-in-law, Tom Buchanan in CA

*My In-laws,
Tom & Neva Buchanan*

*Derl, mother Nellie,
and brother Berl Horn, Jr.*

6

VIETNAM BOUND

I took leave from duty to bring Marilyn back to Camp Lejeune. For the five and one half months I had been in Cuba, we had been checking the days off the calendar, anticipating the day we would be back together again. The reunion was sweet, and we enjoyed our time together at home in Arkansas before traveling back to Camp Lejeune. At this point, we didn't know it would only be another short stay. I only had twelve months left to serve in the Marine Corps, and a typical tour in Vietnam lasted thirteen months. The company commander had mentioned that I would be assigned either stateside or somewhere overseas other than Vietnam. He was convinced that I didn't have enough time for a Vietnam tour. Whatever the assignment would be, I would not complain because in either place, I hoped Marilyn would be able to join me.

Five weeks after we settled back into our apartment, the bad news arrived—orders for Vietnam. I was severely disappointed and a bit angry, but I felt a sense of duty to my country and was committed and willing to serve. Marilyn, on the other hand, was devastated and terrified, realizing that I faced the danger of severe injury or death. We could not imagine the months of separation with the fear that I could be killed hanging over us. We prayed for peace and comfort, realizing we both would have to place our faith and trust in God to protect me in that very dangerous place. As young Christians, we were in the early stages of learning how to leave our anxiety and fear in the Lord's hands. We knew He would be our courage and strength through those difficult months.

We packed up our little Chevy II and headed back home to enjoy a two-week leave, visiting our families and friends before I reported in at El Toro, California. Finally, it was time to leave for Tulsa to catch my flight. As we drove out of town, we passed a Holiday Inn billboard that read, "Good-bye, Derl, our prayers are with you." I was touched and blessed to know our friends had arranged this farewell message to remind me that they would be praying while I was gone.

Marilyn and I spent two days in Tulsa, treasuring each moment. The hours raced by as we tried to forget we would soon be separated. With tears and heavy hearts, we hugged and kissed good-bye at the airport, knowing we would not see each other again for eleven months. I boarded the plane, and as it taxied down the runway, I looked out the window and could see my sweet wife waving from the terminal window. I would carry that picture with me in the difficult months ahead. It was a painful separation, knowing I would not see her for almost a year—and possibly never again. As the plane lifted off the ground, we came close to having a mid-air collision with another plane coming in for landing. The plane was so close I thought it might come in the window I was watching from. It was a scary moment, but it was only the first of many close calls I would encounter during the next year.

Marilyn: Derl and I spent the last few hours tightly holding on to each other, engulfed in a cloud of heaviness. We knew it would be a long time before we were together again, but also that he might never return. Images of the war were on the morning and evening news every day, and I could not escape the reality of what we might face. I realized how difficult it was to convey what was in my heart. I dearly loved him, but I was finding it hard to express my love in those last few moments. It was a struggle to say good-bye because of the emotions welling up inside of me. After kissing him one last time, I watched him walk down the long hallway to the plane. Then I stood at the window to watch the plane depart. I felt very alone, yet I knew God was with me just as He was with Derl. He would walk with us through this difficult journey. My tears flowed as I watched the plane taxi away.

At Camp Horno, I received my final training before leaving for Vietnam. The training areas were set up as reproductions of Vietnamese villages, very similar to what I would find when I arrived in South Vietnam. Marines dressed up in typical Vietnamese clothing, such as long black shirts and the conical straw hats called *non la*. They attempted to look like the local Vietnamese families that lived in the villages alongside our enemy, the Viet Cong. They looked the part and were hiding in the villages as well as in the jungle. Experienced Korean and Vietnam War veterans trained us to recognize and kill the enemy. Their experience would be vital in preparing us for the war ahead.

While at Camp Horno, we filled out the necessary documents for our deployment, composed a last letter to be given to our family in the case of our death, and wrote out our Last Will and Testament. These documents were necessary, but it had a sobering effect on each of us as we realized that some of us would not be coming home.

The next step was immunizations; we were given twenty-five injections. We lined up to walk single file between the nurses with injection guns. Then we were instructed to hold our arms still with no jerking because our arms could be cut by the gun. The most painful shot of the day was the gamma globulin to give our immune systems a boost, helping us fight infections and diseases. It was injected into the cheek of our butt. Once the medicine entered my blood stream I could feel the burning warmth moving throughout my body. Occasionally the corpsman would hit someone's sciatic nerve. This was very painful and caused some of the men to limp for several days. Fortunately it did not happen to me.

Marilyn called to tell me that she was pregnant. I was going to be a daddy! We were both excited, but sad that I couldn't experience the pregnancy with her. Again we were reminded that I might not return to see or be a part of raising our child; I did not let myself think long about that possibility. All I could do for now was look forward to the weekends when I could telephone Marilyn to hear her voice and tell her again how much I loved her.

Marilyn: *After a visit to Dr. James Mashburn on April 19, 1967, he confirmed that I was pregnant! I was experiencing morning sickness, so I was almost certain, but it was good to finally know for sure. I was thrilled to tell Derl and the rest of our family. It was bittersweet news because Derl would be gone for all of the pregnancy and birth. The baby would be two-and-a-half months old before he would be home, but we were both very excited. This little life gave us both something to focus on other than the war. Sometimes the scary thought that I* *might be raising a baby alone would flash through my mind, but I refused to allow myself to go down that road.*

Near the end of April, we realized that we only had a few more days before Derl would leave for Okinawa. Each phone call brought new tension, knowing that it could be our last phone visit for six to ten months. We enjoyed talking about the baby and our future as a family. Derl called his family to let them know I was pregnant and, of course, they were thrilled. We were both very homesick, knowing that we had months of separation ahead and there would be no weekly phone calls. But in just a few days we would be turning the calendar over for the month of May. It helped to mark the days off the calendar I kept by my bedside.

A few weekends before I left for Vietnam, I met my brother-in-law Tommy, who was in training nearby at Camp Pendleton. We were excited to see each other when we met in Oceanside. It felt like a touch of family and home. We found a place to stay, called our family back home, relaxed on the beach, and made trips to the USO club to eat hamburgers. All our conversation centered on family and home as we tried not to think about what was ahead for me.

On May 3, 1967 my Vietnam training was complete, and I was transferred from Camp Horno to the El Toro Marine Corps Air Base. The next day, I flew from El Toro to Okinawa, Japan, to be assigned to a division for Vietnam. It was a long flight over the ocean to Hawaii where we stopped for a couple of hours to refuel the monster Continental 720B Fan Jet. We landed at night and were only allowed in the terminal area. I couldn't see much of the island, but I could say I had visited Hawaii. After another long flight, the plane finally landed in Okinawa.

Okinawa is surrounded by beautiful ocean. From the air it looked like a vacation resort, but that would certainly not describe our camp. I expected Okinawa to be a brief stay, but instead, I ended up being attached to a casual company consisting of Marines waiting for a final assignment to Vietnam.

Every day we were called from our barracks to stand at attention as the names of those selected for Vietnam were read. Those who were not selected to fly out were assigned work details or more training. Each long wait reminded me of the days of waiting to hear from the draft board. I was ready to go and anxious to get the job done.

In the evenings, I enjoyed my free time, chatting with friends I had met earlier while stationed in California and Cuba, friends like Robert Tilbert, Mike Hawn, Ron Kist, Morris Sears, and Dan Hoel. I made many new friends while waiting to be assigned, but most of us would be split up after arriving in-country Vietnam.

Most of the guys spent their evenings and weekend liberty going into the small town that consisted of mostly bars, restaurants, and "cathouses" (brothels). They were interested in satisfying their physical desires, but that was not for me. I loved my wife and had vowed before God to be a faithful husband. When I was in town with my friends, I got harassed and teased a lot as they tried to persuade me to join them, saying, "Come on, she will never know." But God knew, and I did not want to sin against Him. I spent most of my free time going to the movies, eating out, or enjoying the beach.

While in Okinawa, my birthday on May 8 was the hardest day for me. There was not much celebrating for me; in fact, it was the loneliest birthday I could remember. I know God understood how sad and lonely I was, and He sent me the encouragement I needed during mail call, a sweet birthday card from Marilyn. It was a bittersweet moment. The card was precious and made my day better just hearing from her. It also caused me to miss her more, since I would not see her again for almost a year

"Saying Good-bye"

Last night at home

Departing Tulsa International Airport

7

VIETNAM THE REALITY

The day of departure had finally arrived. My name was called to be on a flight at 0630 hours on the morning of June 2, 1967. I was on my way. As we prepared to depart, we were placed in groups of fifty or seventy men. I assumed we were grouped in that manner to make a full load for the C-130 Hercules used for transporting supplies and Marines to Vietnam. The plane was capable of carrying seventy paratroopers and landing on a short dirt runway.

As we arrived at the air terminal to depart, the C-130 was landing on the tarmac, and we were told to wait until it was unloaded. I noticed that large, black bags were being unloaded from the plane. I asked the men standing around what they were unloading; they explained that the black bags contained the remains of the dead we were replacing. I had a terrible sinking feeling with the sharp pain of reality that some of us standing ready to board this plane would also be returning in body bags. I began to pray, crying out to God to remove my fear and to give me courage. When the unloading was finished, we were allowed to board the plane with our sea bags and prepare for the flight. We were packed into the plane for a hot and bumpy ride. The thought and smell of death still lingered inside the plane.

We arrived in Da Nang that afternoon. From first glance, Vietnam was a picturesque land. Impressive mountain ranges formed a backdrop for the fertile coastal plain that once made this tropical country a leading exporter of rice. Bordered by Laos and Cambodia to the west and the South China Sea to the east, this struggling land in Southeast Asia measured approximately sixty-seven thousand square miles, a small space for its sixteen million people.

We unloaded and waited around to check in and get our assignments. We stored our sea bags with our personal belongings, uniforms, and other items that would not be needed again until the end of our tour. We were ready to travel to the forward Marine Corps base near the little village of Dong Ha as soon as the next C-130 was available to transport us.

After a five-hour wait, we were loaded and on our way. The land we saw from our plane windows looked like a piece of Swiss cheese because of all the bomb craters. It was dark when we landed. I thought for sure we were crashing because the landing was so rough that we were thrown out of our seats. I didn't understand why it was so rough until the next morning when I saw the landing strip was made up of layers of sheet metal placed end to end to make a temporary landing strip.

We were hustled off the C-130 Hercules cargo plane to temporary sleeping quarters. The air was humid, hot, and stale, and reeked of aircraft fuel. We were instructed by Marines in charge not to have any kind of light because it would give the enemy a good target. It was so dark we couldn't see anything, causing us to stumble over each other. Once we settled in for the night, none of us were able to sleep for the fear and anxiety of the unknown. Those feelings would never be forgotten. All night we could hear explosions and feel the vibrations as we huddled against the sandbagged walls of the dirt floor bunker.

The next morning, we were trucked out and dumped outside Dong Ha, located in the Quang Tri province about ten miles south of the Demilitarized Zone (DMZ). We were ordered to walk the remaining couple of miles. Vietnam's Demilitarized Zone, established in 1954 at the Geneva conference, divided Vietnam from the former French colony of Indochina. It was intended as a temporary divide, a six-mile-wide buffer zone between the rival governments in the north and south of the country. However, the DMZ became the permanent border between North and South Vietnam.

Dong Ha was to be our headquarters. The location was strategically chosen at the junction of Highway One, running north and south up the coast, and Highway Nine, running east and west to the Laotian border. The terrain in this area of Vietnam varied from rugged mountains to gently rolling sand dunes and rice paddies to a leech-infested triple-canopy jungle. The thick vegetation of the jungle grew at three levels, often reaching up more than fifty feet.

As we entered camp at Dong Ha, we found a complex filled with tattered, windblown tents, trench lines, underground bunkers, and heavily sandbagged artillery positions. Dust and dirt filled the air around us. This area was within rocket range of the DMZ, so everyone moved with great care around the base.

We walked up to a group of Marines, sitting around in their faded battle utilities (Vietnam jungle combat uniforms). Their battle-weary faces stared at us like we were new recruits just out of boot camp. Our bright green utilities made it obvious that we were the new replacements.

I noticed a group of the men sitting around a large, two-foot-square block of ice, chipping off pieces with their bayonets and eating them as a way to cool themselves in the steaming 120- degree heat. They invited us to join them, allowing us to cool off a bit. These men had pooled their money to purchase the ice from the local Vietnamese. I wondered where they had gotten the water to freeze the ice. We had no idea if the ice was clean, but anything cold was a treat.

The men began to share their war stories about previous battles and how they had recently lost half of Bravo Company. I learned that I was a replacement Marine for Bravo Company, also known as "The Walking Dead."[1]

While I was in Vietnam, the North Vietnamese Army (NVA) offered a bounty for the heads of any Bravo 1/9 Marine because of the havoc and death this battalion had caused. We saw pamphlets dropped across the northern area promising rewards for our lives. The enemy hoped to discourage and frighten us with their

---

[1] During the Vietnam War, the unit earned the name "The Walking Dead" for its high casualty rate.[3] The battalion endured the longest sustained combat and suffered the highest killed in action (KIA) rate in Marine Corps history, especially during the Battle of July Two. The battalion was engaged in combat for 47 months and 7 days, from 15 June 1965 to 19 October 1966 and 11 December 1966 to 14 July 1969. Based on a typical battalion strength of 800 Marines and Navy hospital corpsmen, 93.63% (747) were Killed in Action (KIA) and 0.25% (2) were Missing In Action (MIA). From Wikipedia, the free encyclopedia.

propaganda while, at the same time, encouraging their soldiers to fight harder.

Our first job was filling and stacking sandbags around bunkers and trenches. We became hot and dirty from many trips into the bush to fill the sandbags, so we were ordered to take a shower. The showers were crude PVC pipes connected together in the wide-open spaces. Holes were pierced in them to allow the water to spray out. The water felt good on my skin with the temperature being so hot. It was a strange feeling to shower stark naked in front of twenty or more men with nothing between you and the sky. This contraption was a poor excuse for a shower, but I soon learned that showers would be few and far between for the rest of my tour.

That evening, I had a moment to write my first letter home to Marilyn, letting her know that I had arrived safely and how much I missed her. I explained our time difference. I was fifteen hours ahead of the time back home. At that moment, home seemed a million miles away. The next few weeks were emotionally tough since I did not receive mail from Marilyn or anyone else. Because I was in transition, moving to different locations, it took three to five weeks before the mail caught up with me.

The next morning, June 3rd, I was assigned to Bravo 1/9, 3rd Division, the 60mm mortar section and issued my Geneva Convention card. This card contained my name, rank, and date of birth, as well as the internationally agreed upon rights of the treatment of prisoners of war during captivity. I was also issued my 782 field gear: rifle, ammo, flak jacket, poncho, poncho liner, grenades, bayonet, e-tool (small shovel), two canteens, Halazone tablets for water purification, malaria prevention tabs and enough C-rations to last three to four days.

My MOS (Military Occupational Specialty) was mortars. I had trained to fire 81mm mortars, only to be informed that there was no need here for an 81mm mortar man. Instead I was assigned to the 60mm mortar section of Bravo Company, handed a compass and a map, and told that I would be helping plot our routes and determine the locations to fire the mortars. I thought, *Here we go again, another promise broken.* I had assured Marilyn that I would be assigned to fire the 81mm mortars, providing firepower from behind the actual combat zone. The 60mm mortars traveled with the rifle company between platoons. I was not only responsible for plotting the directions to fire the mortars, but also helping set up the mortars and zero them in on the target point. I had also assured Marilyn I would not be responsible for geographical directions. This was a concern for her since she knew I was "directionally challenged," meaning I get lost easily. Now I found myself responsible for giving directions to our mortar squad as to where to fire the mortar.

I was an E-3 Lance Corporal and would be an ammo carrier for a few days before becoming the 60mm mortar assistant gunner. Specifically, I would carry a rifle along with the tripods for the mortar. The tripod, with its wide legs, was a bulky piece of equipment to carry along with my rifle, but I didn't complain because I felt much safer having these weapons to defend myself.

Derl at Camp Carroll, Vietnam

*Back: Richard Knee, unknown, Tom Hines,
John Gunning, Derl Horn, unknown. Front: Walt Meekings*

8

READY FOR ACTION

I was in the jungles of Vietnam and ready for action. My mortar section consisted of two mortars with four men per mortar squad, plus a section leader. Normally, a section leader would have been a 1st or 2nd lieutenant but there was a shortage of lieutenants. My mortar squad was assigned to the weapons platoon under Sgt. Richard Huff. My gunner was Corporal Coulee, a funny, seasoned short-timer also from Arkansas. Our squad leader was Corporal Prichard, a calm and cool Marine from Oklahoma who was also a short-timer. He gave me some good advice about the enemy mortars and rockets. He once told me, "If you hear them, they are going over your head. If you don't hear them, they could be in your foxhole with you."

I was glad to be with some good-old southern boys. Corporal Coulee was impressive. Instead of the usual military holster, he wore a western belt holster tied to his leg, carrying his .45-caliber pistol. His belt was lined with bullets. All he needed was a cowboy hat! The gunner always carried a .45-caliber pistol instead of a rifle because it was too difficult to carry the barrel of the mortar attached to the base plate and a rifle. We each carried six to eight rounds of ammo for the mortar along with our other ammo and personal gear, including our helmets and flak jackets. The rounds weighed around three pounds each, so we were packing seventy-five to eighty pounds of weight. I lost twenty pounds in the first few weeks from the combination of extreme heat and carrying such a heavy load.

Blood, Sweat and Honor

My mortar section was attached to Bravo Company, and my squad was attached to the First Rifle Platoon. We were given orders for a search and destroy mission in the Quang Tri Province. We headed out early in the morning of June 6, 1967. My first day in the field was both exciting and scary. We were on the move for most of the day, crossing streams, hills, and jungle areas. We were just coming into a clearing when we heard several large booms. The experienced Marines yelled, "Incoming!" which meant just that, mortars or rockets were coming in directly on top of us. The mortars pounded the ground all around us and we ran for cover into the tree lines, looking for low places to jump into. My heart was racing and the adrenaline flooded my nervous system as I experienced my first day of combat. After several minutes of mortars exploding, it was quiet again. Fortunately, none of us were hurt. Later we heard on the radio that there had been a mix-up and we were being mortared by our own men. We continued to march on with caution after that incident.

It was almost dark before we found a good place to dig foxholes and set up our perimeter for the night. In our mortar section, we dug two-man foxholes large enough for two men and a mortar to be set up and ready to fire. That was the routine throughout most of my tour in Vietnam: move during the day and dig a home for the night. I learned to love the safety of my foxhole after a few firefights because I was a lot safer below the ground avoiding rifle rounds, projectile explosions, and shrapnel flying through the air.

My first night in the field during Operation Cimarron was sleepless. This operation was a land-clearing project intended to destroy enemy bunkers and supply caches. I was listening to the weathered veterans share their stories and advice on how to stay alive. I paid close attention and tried to absorb all they had to say. I knew that my wife and family back home were praying for me, but I also knew I had to be smart, careful, and do my part. Several in the group shared how they had already been struck once or twice with only minor wounds. If a serviceman sustained three combat wounds, he would be sent home no matter how minor they were. Some of the wounded men were hoping for a third, small, insignificant wound. They wanted to go home. After already being in the field for nine to twelve months, they were exhausted.

DERL HORN

Have no fear of sudden disaster or of the ruin that overtakes the wicked, for the Lord will be at your side and will keep your foot from being snared.
(Proverbs 3:25-26 NIV)

On my second day in the field, I was up before daylight. We ate our C-ration breakfast[2], covered up our foxholes, and headed out. Everything was going well until around noon when we walked into a squad-sized Viet Cong (VC) ambush. The VC was a grouping of guerrilla fighters who fought against both the government of South Vietnam and the Armed Forces of the United States. They were using command-detonated, claymore-type mines and automatic small arms. Without a place or time to set up our mortars, we all took cover and began returning rifle fire to the bush line where the enemy was firing from. We hurried to find a hole to escape into or a tree to hide behind. I ended up in a thickly wooded area, trying to look in every direction at once. The bullets were hitting all around me, making it hard to determine the directions of the shots because of the wooded area.

The VC were good at hiding and waiting on us in their spider holes, which consisted of a man-size burrow dug in the ground. Each spider hole had a tight fitting removable lid made of silk and earth, covered with soil or gravel to disguise the entrance. Along with a couple of my comrades, I finally managed to crawl into a bomb crater. Our squad leader had just sustained shrapnel wounds on his hand. Because of this injury he would receive his third Purple Heart. He was excited at the thought that he would be going home if we could survive the ambush. I was thinking and praying, *Good Lord, how will I ever stay alive if it is going to be like this every day?* Since the enemy was well protected with cover from the tree line, our company commander, Captain Curd, called in air strikes and artillery fire to help clear the tree line. Finally after what seemed like an eternity, the firing and bombing stopped from both sides. We began to crawl out of our holes and emerge from behind trees while we cautiously looked around.

---

[2] Each C-ration contains one canned meat item; one canned fruit, bread or dessert item; one B unit containing a hot chocolate packet and cookies or crackers with cheese or peanut butter; an accessory packet containing cigarettes, matches, chewing gum, toilet paper, coffee, cream, sugar, and salt; and a spoon. Four can openers (P38) are provided in each case of 12 meals.

This fire fight resulted in two dead VC. We lost one Marine KIA (Killed in Action) and eight others were wounded. We probed and checked the bushes and sheds looking for more VC. We flushed out and captured two who were hiding in the bushes. Their faces reflected panic and fear as they looked at us not knowing what would happen next. We treated them with respect but kept them under heavy guard waiting on a decision to be made about what to do with them.

Helicopters were called in to evacuate our wounded and dead along with the two prisoners. As one helicopter lifted and hovered over our position, one of the prisoners fell, his arms and legs flailing as he hit the ground with a thud. He was dead on impact. I could not believe what I had just witnessed. Later we were told the man jumped, but we wondered if the prisoners were being questioned and would not talk so one was thrown out of the helicopter, causing the other prisoner to reveal all he knew.

There was a fundamental difference between us and the NVA. We were fighting to win the battles, and they were committed to driving us out of Vietnam, as they had done with the French a decade and a half earlier. Most of us were trying to survive our thirteen months (or however long we had left in the bush) to return home to the USA—our sane personal world—and to be with our families. The NVA soldiers did not have a rotation or end to their tour date. Many did not even have a home to return to. They were stuck in the war for the duration, knowing that they had to win or die trying.

Marilyn: *The dreaded time had finally arrived. Derl was in Vietnam and in the field, ready for combat. He was not assigned with the 81mm mortars behind the infantry in a safer place, as we had hoped, but with the smaller 60mm mortars accompanying the infantry. The uncertainty of what was happening was difficult. Days went by without letters. Fear was constantly rising up within me. I had to continually remind myself that God was our protection. When the letters finally began to arrive, they were not comforting as I read about the ambushes and fire fights. The question always on my mind was: How will Derl make it for the next ten months?*

John Gunning, unknown and Derl

Vietnam

Derl at Camp Carroll, Vietnam

9
OPERATION CIMARRON IN QUANG TRI PROVINCE

On June 10th our 2nd Platoon surprised an NVA ambush site. As they engaged the enemy, we supported them with our 60mm mortars and helped to destroy the ambush. This platoon also found and disarmed five claymore mines and multiple chicom mines that were rigged to explode. They captured one NVA, killed one and possibly one other. The NVA tried to hide their dead, but as they dragged them off, they left a trail of blood. Two of our men who sustained light shrapnel wounds received medical attention and were able to stay in the field.

Our company was assigned to protect the 11th Engineers and all their equipment as they cleared a 600-meter strip between Con Thien and Gio Linh. The Engineers were available to build whatever the combat forces needed at the time. In this case, they built a planned firebreak buffer zone spanning the entire length of the DMZ with six strong points and twelve watchtowers. The Engineers and Navy Seabees were impressive in all they were able to accomplish while in Vietnam. They supported the troops, and we, in turn, were their protection. They built roads, airfields, warehouses, hospitals, storage facilities, and bunkers in critical areas such as Quang Tri, Thua Thien, Quang Nam, Quang In, and Quang Ngai. They had a very hot and dirty assignment with all the heavy equipment used for moving dirt and trees. All their equipment was shipped by naval vessels and then air lifted into position by huge cargo planes. We patrolled the buffer strip to protect them as they built different structures during the day. We set up camp nearby each night, depending on the location of our patrols along the strip during the day.

On the second day, we encountered the VC from a distance. They were attempting to infiltrate the perimeter. At that point, Navy air strikes were called in to take them out. The VC fired mortar rounds and small arms fire to distract us, but when the air strikes began, their firing stopped.

For the first few days in this area, the weather was partly cloudy. It felt good to hide from the relentless sun for short periods of time. It rained in the evenings, leaving us wet and too uncomfortable to sleep. The nights were already short after long days of marching, followed by rotating watches of three to five hours throughout the night. It made for a physically and mentally exhausted Marine the next morning.

One evening after my watch, I curled up in an old mortar crater and went to sleep until early morning. When I woke up and rolled over, I discovered that the hole had filled with water from rain during the night. I had been so tired that I had not heard or felt the rain. Everything I was wearing was soaked, including my smokes. After that night, I learned to place anything of value in a plastic bag to keep it dry.

The next day we spotted some VC hiding in the nearby tree lines, so we fired several mortar rounds in that vicinity to disrupt any attacks they had planned. One platoon was sent out to survey the area and found two dead VC and captured one. We continued to fire mortar rounds outside our perimeter to discourage the VC and to lighten the heavy load on our backs. It was difficult to carry more than six rounds of ammunition per man with all the other gear we carried. The load was heavy and tiring as we constantly moved up and down the strip. I realized early on that my pack was just too heavy, so I discarded unnecessary items like tents and blankets. I only carried a poncho and poncho liner for my bedding. It did not take long for me to realize I should only carry the necessities: food, water, toothbrush, razor, letter-writing materials, grenades, ammo and an entrenching tool--the lighter the load, the better. The men in my mortar section still carried eighty to one-hundred pounds of weight, not including a helmet, a flak jacket, and something we were never without—a weapon.

I was adjusting to eating C-rations; there were some I preferred over others. We would trade C-rations back and forth to get the ones we enjoyed. I learned to drink that gosh-awful "C-rat" coffee, and, believe it or not, there even came a day when I liked it. I would use my heat tab, a flammable fuel tablet about the size of half-dollar, to heat my coffee, and then I would eat cold C-rations.

I had only been in the field for ten days, but with all the battles I had already faced, I felt like a seasoned combat Marine.

The heat was unbearable and the construction dust mixed with sweat made me miserable. I really needed a bath and a shave. We came upon a crater about the size of a livestock pond, formed by a large bomb. It was half-full of water, so we decided to bathe in the crater. We took turns guarding and then bathing. It felt good to wash off all the dirt and splash around in the water. The only problem was climbing out of the hole. The sides were slick and muddy, making it difficult to come out completely clean. But it was refreshing to be free of the layers of dirt and sweat, if only for a short time. With a week's worth of growth on my face, shaving was difficult using just body soap and a dull razor, but it felt good to be clean even for just a day.

We spent our days protecting the strip and trying to stay cool. We used our ponchos and dead tree limbs to make a shield from the sun while we rested and wrote to family and friends back home. I had not received any letters and was anxiously awaiting one from Marilyn. In the far-away jungle, letters from home were our lifeline. It was hard to believe I was so lonely in the middle of a company of men. My faith in Christ helped me through the gloomy times as I trusted Him to guide me.

We constantly stayed on the alert because of the mortars, rockets, and small-arms fire that harassed us daily. Sometimes the enemy mortars would get lucky. At one point, they hit an Amtrak used for moving heavy loads, wounding two of our Marines.

On June 18, 1967, the 11th Engineering Unit completed the job of widening the strip to Gio Linh. Our mission changed from guarding the strip to conducting search and destroy sweeps. During these sweeps we discovered numerous booby traps and fighting positions that we destroyed with grenades and explosives. We were under constant enemy harassment with mortars and sniper fire.

It was a sad day when one of our Marines was killed with his own .45 caliber pistol. No one was sure what happened, but some speculated that he had been cleaning the gun or playing with it while it was loaded. It was depressing to realize that not only did we have the VC trying to kill us, but we were a danger to ourselves if we were tired or careless.

In a letter, I shared with Marilyn that I had decided to adjust and accept the way things were in the jungle for the next nine months. My attitude was to make the best of it, and I was making progress. I started out as 1st ammo humper and after a couple of days, I was promoted to assistant gunner. Then after two weeks I was moved into the gunner position. My promotions were a result of fellow Marines being killed, wounded, or transferred home. My section leader informed me that a third mortar had been ordered, and I would be the squad leader when it arrived

10
LETTERS FROM HOME

Some days in Vietnam passed quickly with lots of action, while other days dragged by slowly, feeling like an eternity. I had been in the field for sixteen days when I finally received two letters from Marilyn. It was a relief to know she and the baby were doing well. She still worked part time at a steak house, and the transition to living at home with her parents again was "smooth" but hard. We had been married just three years and loved each other deeply; however, the separation and adjustment were difficult.

In the following days, I received more letters from Marilyn, my parents, and some friends back home. It was encouraging to hear about their activities because even the little day-to-day things that may seem unimportant to them were important to me. I felt like I was losing touch with normal life, fighting the daily battles that were so foreign to my life back home. My letters were repetitious, expressing my love for my wife over and over, always keeping in mind it might be my last message to her. I had constant concern and worry for her health and our baby she was carrying. I did not want her to worry about my safety, so I assured her that I was okay and not to worry. I know those words felt empty as the TV news coverage told a different story. I would think about her and how she would change through the pregnancy. It was hard to imagine her with a growing belly since she had always been slim and trim. It was sweet to dream about the baby we would have and what he or she would look like. As I sat in the jungle, it was almost impossible to believe that one day we would be a family of three.

I realized that Vietnam was a narrowly focused war and as "grunts" (combat infantry), we would never understand the big picture, even years later when our government stopped a war that we could have won. All we could see and understand at that time was the jungle we moved through and the holes we dug each night. We were moving targets as we sloshed through rice patties and bamboo thickets.

As we walked through the country, we encountered skinny pigs much like our Arkansas razorbacks, ugly chickens, and naked kids. We watched as men and women wearing pointed straw hats and black pants guided black water buffalo to work the fields. They seemed to ignore the war around them. At night many of them would lay down their plows and take up weapons against us. It made me wonder what kind of a place Vietnam was and what this war was about. I saw all kinds of people; some of the women were beautiful until they flashed a smile to reveal black teeth that appeared rotten from chewing betel nut. The betel nut was a small fruit of the areca palm. Chewing it was a Vietnamese custom, much like chewing tobacco or gum in the States, but it caused their lips and mouths to turn red and their teeth appeared to have a black coating on them.

It was a sad and scary time for the Vietnamese people, as well as for those of us who were separated from our loved ones and doing our best to defend them and fight for their freedom.

11
CON THIEN, "THE HILL OF ANGELS"

Our next assignment was at Con Thien; our mission was to occupy and defend the base. We arrived late one afternoon in time to establish a perimeter and set up our mortars before dark. Con Thien is a hill 158 meters high, surrounded by a cluster of three small hills, and large enough to accommodate a reinforced battalion. The area is an ugly, bare patch of red mud called "The Hill of Angels" by local missionaries because of the large number of battle casualties. Con Thien was considered an important stronghold, and our mission was to defend the hill and to defeat the NVA's attempts to move south. The men who served at Con Thien had given it a few nicknames, such as "The Meat Grinder," "The Target," and "Our Turn in the Barrel." While on the hill, we received at least 200 mortar and rocket rounds daily. Ammunition was supplied to the NVA from the Soviets and Red Chinese. During my three stays on the hill, I don't remember a day that we did not receive incoming rounds of some kind.

The constant mortar and rocket pounding at Con Thien created unbelievable stress. We were all about to go nuts, and some of the men did experience nervous breakdowns. It was difficult surviving in the middle of a war zone with the constant fear of not knowing if the next round had your name on it. We battled hard to even up the score by firing our mortars day and night at the NVA, dropping a barrage of mortars wherever there was indication of any NVA activity. We defended our perimeter with very little sleep because of the continual firing and being fired upon. It truly felt like we were indeed taking turns in a barrel as the NVA pounded us for a couple of hours, and then we pounded them. They were good at camouflaging their location, and they did most of their firing in the late afternoon when the muzzle flashes were difficult to see.

The NVA had us in their cross-hairs on this "Hill of Angels," killing Marines daily as we attempted to defend ourselves and to destroy them as they moved outside our perimeter. It was exciting on occasions to see a secondary explosion after dropping our mortars into their location. The explosion let us know we had destroyed their ammo storage dump and possibly killed several "gooks," [3] Each time a helicopter landed on our base to resupply us or to pick up our dead and wounded, it gave the enemy a target and they dropped a barrage of rocket and mortar rounds on us. The battle never let up, and we constantly defended Con Thien with our mortars and M-16 rifles. We worked hard to keep the enemy off our hill.

It was a risky job on the hill with Marines being killed and wounded daily. The rewards were few and the pay was not so great. As a Lance Corporal, I received $122.00 a month plus $65.00 hazardous duty combat pay for a whopping total of $187.00 per month or $2,244.00 per year. Clearly we were not serving in this war for the money. We continued to occupy Con Thien and defend the base for five more days before we began our next mission, Operation Buffalo.

I did not receive many letters while at Con Thien, and I was very homesick. Marilyn, my family, and home were all I could think about in my free time. I shared with the guys a dream about receiving a lot of mail from home. Later that day during mail call, to my surprise, I received eleven letters. None of us could believe that my dream had come true. Letters from home were morale boosters. In this batch of letters I heard from most of my family—my mom, dad, sister, brother-in-law, and four good friends. The rest of the letters were from Marilyn. One of her letters, sent for my birthday in early May, arrived seven weeks late. I was excited to find a picture of her in one of her first maternity dresses. She was beautiful, and I longed to be with her. She shared with me about her doctor's visits and how our baby was growing and had a strong heartbeat. She was also feeling the baby move. I was so excited, desperately wanting to be there with

---

[3] Negative slang term for Viet Cong.

her. It was hard for me to comprehend the changes taking place and that I would be a daddy in five months. Our baby's due date was November 26, 1967. How could I stand not being there for the birth? I continued to trust God and depend on Him for my safety, as well as a safe delivery for Marilyn and our baby.

The rain continually made a muddy mess out of everything we touched; we could not get away from the red clay. We were filthy dirty without a way to stay clean. I was thankful our mortar section was stationed in one location while the grunt units were going out on patrols and ambushes. However, I knew it would not be long before we would be taking our turn out in the field with the company patrols and ambushes.

Finally the rain stopped, and the sun beat down on us at a sweltering 115 degrees. The humidity was unbearable—much worse than the hot, humid summers back home.

***The Lord is with me: I will not be afraid.
What can man do to me? The Lord is with me; He is my helper. I will look in triumph on my enemies.
(Psalm 118:6-7 NIV)***

Digging one of many foxholes

12
OPERATION BUFFALO

In July of 1967, 1st Battalion, 9th Marines commanded by Lieutenant Colonel Richard J. Schening took part in Operation Buffalo in and around Con Thien, having been ordered to defend Con Thien and the border between North and South Vietnam, known as the Demilitarized Zone (DMZ). This province was the scene of some of the fiercest ground fighting during the Vietnam War. Companies A and B operated north of the former market place on Route 561. We were to sweep the area just 1200 yards east of Con Thien and north of the Trace (space that had been cleared out between the DMZ and South Vietnam) in an attempt to drive out and keep the NVA from settling into the area, which would threaten our Con Thien stronghold. Company D under the command of Captain Sasek, Headquarters and Service Company and the Battalion Command Group remained within the outpost perimeter. Company C under command of Captain Hutchison was to remain at Dong Ha under Colonel George Jerue's 9th Marines command post.

As part of Bravo Company, we left Con Thien the morning of June 30, 1967 at 0900. As my company prepared to leave, Capt. Sterling Coates approached us with a final word. He told us five battalions of NVA were somewhere along the DMZ. He warned us to be careful. My heart began to pound as I realized there might be as many as 5,000 enemy soldiers. Captain Coates ended the conversation with an attempt to reassure us, saying, "We are not likely to see any of them."

Blood, Sweat and Honor

I was thinking, *I am still a boot* (new guy) *in Vietnam with only a month in country*. I was overcome with a heavy, sick, scared feeling in my stomach just thinking about the possibilities of encountering any of the 5,000 NVA with our company of only 150 men. We were already fifty men short of a full company. This made us feel somewhat edgy, since our company had just been reassembled after losing half of our men during the Khe Sanh battles in April. As the captain talked, I knew these were not good odds. I looked around at the other men, wondering if they felt the same way I did. We tried not to show fear, but as we left Con Thien, I found myself praying, "*Dear God, please protect us and give us courage.*"

Walking slowly and carefully, we started our sweep and traveled a couple of miles from Con Thien along the Quang Tri Province, the geographic center of Vietnam, extending from the South China Sea to Laos. We settled on a location between two tree lines to dig in and set up our perimeter for the night. Patrols were sent out to locate and destroy any NVA positions. Only one position was discovered and blown up with composition C-4, a demolition charge packed in a mylar-wrapped container. A pressure sensitive adhesive strip on one side allowed it to be affixed to any clean, dry, non-frozen surface.

Oddly enough, we found other, non-destructive uses for the C-4, such as heating our coffee and C-rations. A small portion worked perfectly when broken off, rolled into a ball, and then set on fire. However, it could never be used at night because the light from the fire made us a target for the enemy, and we might find ourselves eating bullets instead of rations.

After I dug in for the night, I spread my poncho and poncho liner on the hard ground next to my foxhole and tried to get some sleep. My only opportunity for sleep would be between watches, and I needed to get to sleep quickly to be rested for my watch. But knowing a large number of the enemy were nearby made it hard to close my eyes. Hearing the restless movements of the other men reminded me I was not alone. We were all facing the same fear. I wondered if any of us would be able to sleep.

The next morning I packed my gear, pulled out my e-tool, and filled my fox hole with dirt. With the first crack of daylight we were back on the trail, walking with a space of ten yards between us to keep from attracting the enemy's attention.

About midmorning, we came upon an abandoned enemy

bunker. Someone felt the ashes and realized they were still warm, meaning the enemy had not been gone long. The bunker was destroyed with a block of C-4, and we continued moving north toward the DMZ. We soon came upon a small village that seemed deserted until someone noticed villagers behind a hut. Our point Marines were sent to observe and check out the village. It felt like an eternity as we waited in suspense. The air was humid and hot, causing sweat beads to form and run down my neck. It was hard not to swat the gnats and mosquitoes swarming around my head.

As I waited near a bush, I noticed movement in the elephant grass about fifteen yards to my right. As I watched, a large snake appeared. It was around eight to ten feet long, and its head was much larger than its body. I did not know what it was but suspected that it might be a Monocellate, or King Cobra, since they can grow up to eighteen feet long and are very venomous. I was afraid this might be the snake Marines call "Two-Step," given because, after a bite, the victim could only take two steps before he died. The snake raised his head above the grass and looked around. He then seemed to fix his eyes on me and headed in my direction. I knew I could not fire my weapon without giving away our position, so I drew my bayonet to kill him before he could bite me. He continued to slither closer. When he got within ten feet of me, he stopped, looked at me, turned, and headed in the opposite direction. I let out a deep sigh of relief and wondered what would have happened if that snake had not turned around. I had been told there were 140 snake species in Vietnam and thirty of them were poisonous. My thinking was that the only good snake is a dead snake.

In Vietnam, the NVA and VC were not our only enemies. As we tried to stay alive, we were in a constant battle against sunburn; chapped, cracked lips and noses; twisted ankles; dehydration; diarrhea; and joint and muscle pains from humping (carrying) our heavy packs. Other serious problems included heat, hunger, malaria, spreading jungle rot, poisonous snakes, scorpions, huge biting ants and centipedes, along with the threat of tigers. We lived in continual fear of injury and death, the terror of ambush, overwhelming exhaustion, and the nagging doubt that this war would ever end. We also fought against boredom and the fear of letting our guard down.

Captain Coates finally gave us the okay to proceed into the village. As we entered, we first searched the bombed-out buildings, only to find a couple of elderly Vietnamese women and some children. Then to our horror, we saw body parts lying around and realized there had been a fierce battle with explosives. The odor was horrible….so bad you could taste it. The smell of death is the worst kind of stench, impossible to remove from your nostrils or your memory.

As we inspected a small church, we noticed that the pews were broken and turned over, with clutter all over the floor. There were broken windows, empty shells, and bloody bandages lying around near the windows. I found myself thinking, *This church must have been beautiful before the war.* It was sad to see it torn apart. After making certain there were no VC, we continued on with our search-and-destroy patrol. Once we verified there was nothing else to destroy, we moved down the trail, looking for a safe place to stop for the night.

It had been a busy, stressful day, and we were exhausted by the time we stopped. I had a can of pineapple juice in my pack, a treat sent from home. I opened it, only to find it was too hot to drink. I decided to leave it out overnight to cool so I could enjoy it the next morning.

Wiping sweat and dirt from my face, I prepared to help set up our perimeter and dig foxholes before dark. The darkness began to fall around me as I dug my foxhole. My mind played tricks on me in the dark. As I looked at the trees, I thought I could see someone moving. The bushes seemed to cry out with danger. Although it was an uneventful night, I felt like a constant target. During the night I could hear mortar rounds being fired in the distance. It is hard to explain the intense dread I felt. I realized the enemy was looking for us and firing their mortars at what they thought was our position. None of the mortars landed on us, so we assumed they had miscalculated our position. The events the next day proved us wrong. They were zeroing in on the route they expected us to travel and setting up an ambush. We were on 75 percent watch during the night which meant very little sleep. We knew the enemy was very close.

Though I walk in the mist of trouble, you preserve my life, you stretch out your hand against the anger of my foes, with your right hand you save me.
(Psalm 138:7 NIV)

13

AMBUSH AT THE DMZ

The early morning air was refreshing since it was the coolest part of the hot day. I reached for my pineapple juice and began to chug it down. Something caught between my teeth as I took gulps of the juice. I spit out a grasshopper, then finished drinking. It had been another long night without much sleep, and the sun was up for another hot and humid day. I looked around at all the weary Marines with bloodshot eyes, exhausted after being on alert and watch for most of the night.

We had a quick breakfast of C-rations, threw our trash in our foxholes, and filled them up with dirt to be sure we left nothing of use for the NVA. We left our camping area in the same or better condition than we found it. We loaded our gear and weapons and headed out around 0700 hours on July 2nd. By 0900, we reached and secured a small crossroad about 1200 meters north of the Trace, also referred to as the McNamara line or strip. This line was supposed to be a constructed electronic anti-infiltration barrier below the DMZ. Its purpose was to sound an alarm when the enemy crossed the barrier and to curb infiltration of men and supplies from the North. The barrier was originally planned to be 600 to 1000 meters wide, a stretch of cleared ground containing barbed wire, minefields, sensors, and watchtowers. In reality it was just a long stretch of partially cleared land 600 plus meters wide.

After a two-hour sweep, we moved north along Route 561, an old cart road with waist-high hedgerows on both sides. We heard shots and realized we were under sniper fire. At first we thought it was only a few VC or NVA. Our company commander ordered Sergeant Burns of the 1st Platoon to send out a squad to take care of the enemy. The rest of 1st Platoon was to remain in their overnight position to wait for supplies. The 3rd Platoon went first, followed by the 2nd Platoon, and then Weapons Platoon. Our 60mm mortar section was to continue on up Route 561 in the direction of Con Thien. As we walked, I kept thinking, *We are way too close to the DMZ to be safe*. The order given was for Lance Corporal Herbert's eight-man rifle squad and Cpl Margarito Garza's two-machine gun team to walk point for Bravo's 2nd Platoon. At this point, Staff Sergeant Reyes's 3rd Platoon was leading Bravo Company as we reached an area on Route 561 called the Market Place. All hell broke loose as Reyes's platoon entered into the Market Place. Unknowingly, we had walked into a well-dug, U-shaped ambush by the 3rd Battalion NVA.

Others thought that we had surprised the NVA as they were preparing an attack on Con Thien, but either way, we were in a fierce battle. It was a well-coordinated attack by the NVA battalions, the ones we were not supposed to encounter. The firing on Bravo Company began just beyond the second crossroad at the Market Place. Reyes was the first person shot. We were cut off and surrounded. The 3rd and 2nd Platoons were annihilated almost instantly. Sergeant Huff, the weapons platoon sergeant, screamed for us to get the mortars set up and to return fire. We were already setting up the mortars, so we started dropping them at the trench line as we adjusted elevation and deflection in support of what was left of the two platoons. The NVA mortars and rockets were falling all around us. We attempted to pinpoint their positions to return mortar fire. They were using 82mm mortars and rockets, along with light and medium artillery, while we only had our 60mm mortars. We continually fired mortar rounds back at them and managed to knock out two of their positions. We also received rifle fire and exploding grenades, indicating that the NVA were very close to us.

Bravo Company's 2nd and 3rd Platoons were almost destroyed, leaving only a few of their men along with our mortar squad to battle the enemy. The NVA had done a good job of digging in with spider holes and trenches, along with snipers in the trees. They caught us in a U-shaped crossfire ambush, leaving us with no place to go. We were hit with crisscrossing mortars, rockets, and automatic weapons fire. Suddenly everyone around me was getting hit and dying. Captain Coates radioed Staff Sergeant Burns of 1st Platoon and told him to send part of his platoon forward with machine guns and ammo to support 3rd Platoon; the rest of his platoon was to back up 2nd and Weapons Platoons. Our 81mm mortar forward observer was instructed by Sgt. William Hilliard to call in 81mm mortar support for Bravo's 2nd and 3rd Platoons. The forward observer operating the radio attempted to call, but the radio wasn't transmitting. It could receive but would not transmit.

We were firing our mortars so fast that the mortar barrel was turning red from the increment heat. We removed most of the increments from the fin of the mortar rounds so they would fall short because we were only thirty to fifty meters from the enemy. We managed to hold back the NVA only temporarily because we were so outnumbered. We continued firing our mortars as we adjusted the angle of the tube almost straight up in the air. We could hear screams from the enemy as our mortars hit, so we knew we were doing damage, but not nearly enough. We were being hit by rocks and dirt from our own mortar explosions. We continued to fire our mortars until we were out of rounds. Staff Sergeant Burns had assigned our other mortar squad to fire a mission on Hill 70 which was crawling with NVA.

We were cut off from the other mortar squad and had used up all of our mortar ammo. PFC Tom Hines and I jumped into a bomb crater as we fired our weapons and hurled all the grenades we could find at the NVA. We could hear them coming for us as they screamed and fired their weapons. The dust, dirt, and rocks were so thick from exploding mortars and rockets that we could only see a few feet in front of us. It felt like we were the only ones left because we could not see or hear any of our fellow Marines.

Crack! Crack! The gooks fired their AK-47s all around the crater where we were huddled together. (The AK-47 is a gas-operated automatic rifle with a 30 round banana magazine clip.) I realized that we had a very small chance of survival. Our options were few because we were so outnumbered and about to be overrun. We could stay where we were and be killed or captured and tortured; or we could run and take our chances. My decision was to run. I had to leave behind my mortar and backpack filled with letters, Bible, camera, film, food, and water.

"Tom, I'm going to run. Give me cover." I requested. "When I get to safety, I will cover you." I prayed as I jumped from the crater, "Lord, please protect me and return me home to my family." I began to run, expecting cover from Hines, but as he fired his first shot, his rifle jammed from all the dirt.[4]

With little protection from the gooks, I made my move. They were screaming and throwing grenades, making it difficult to stay on my feet. I could hear the bullets from their rifles landing with a thud around me, tearing up the ground as I ran a zigzag pattern as fast as I could. My only protection was the .45 pistol issued to me as the mortar gunner. I was running for my life, looking for cover and expecting at any moment to suffer the pain of the bullets. I was sprinting through a metal hail storm, but God truly placed His shield of protection around me as I finally reached LCorp Simon Cull and PFC Ronnie Fields from another mortar squad. Together we gave Tom Hines cover as he ran toward us.

Later we learned we were outnumbered thirty to one. We had just faced five NVA Battalions, the ones we were told we would not encounter. As we continued to fight our way back, attempting to reach the Landing Zone (LZ), we found other Marines, making eight Marines. I felt a bit safer even though most of the men were wounded. One of the Marines was my assistant gunner; he had been shot in his side and wrist. He had earlier told me he felt if anyone would survive Vietnam, it would be me. He thought I was a good person because I was a Christian and did not use foul language. He also knew I had a pregnant wife, so he encouraged me to believe I would return home. I tried to encourage him, saying, "We are going to make it out of here."

During my tour in Vietnam, the things that struck the most fear in me were the possibility of being captured and tortured and the fear of losing a limb. I did not want to die, but I was not afraid of death.

At twelve years of age I had prayed to receive Jesus Christ as my Savior and Lord. I knew I had been given eternal life and a place was

---

[4] The M-16 rifle is a good weapon but it had its defects. We were taught that the M-16 rifle would do a good job for you but only if the parts were kept clean. That was not possible in a dirty fire fight. It was later discovered that the M16's excessive malfunctioning was directly related to the type of powder used in the ammunition. It left a residue in the chamber and on the other moving parts that caused pitting. The pits held the expended cartridge tight in the chamber so when a new round was fed into the chamber, it would jam behind the spent cartridge.

reserved for me in heaven. The hardest part was to think about leaving Marilyn and our unborn baby to manage life alone. I did not want her to raise our child as a single mom. Up to this point, my faith had been strong. I felt that God would deliver me from this war, but in the midst of the battle, my faith had wavered. The ambush with crossing mortars, rockets, and automatic weapons had caused the death of many of my fellow Marines, while others sustained traumatic injuries. *It* was a horrendous experience. Many paid the ultimate sacrifice through blood, sweat and honor.

> ***Greater love hath no man than***
> ***this that a man lay down his life for his friends.***
> ***(John 15:13 NIV)***

Our small group spread out and inched our way towards the LZ as the mortar and rocket rounds continued to explode around us with fiery vengeance. We held our helmets tight to our heads to help absorb the impact. Hot metal flew in all directions, tearing and cutting into flesh. The bombing stopped for a few seconds; then we heard the NVA coming our way, screaming and shooting the wounded Marines. Knowing we were outnumbered, we took cover among the tall elephant grass and brush along the winding trail. We had four Marines on each side of the trail and hoped to surprise the NVA before they had an opportunity to kill us. This could be our last stand. I looked up and saw the NVA coming our way with their rifles up and ready as they looked for us.

One soldier walked straight up the trail in our direction. I realized it would not be long before he would see me. He was a huge man, not built like the smaller Vietnamese soldiers but more like the Chinese Regulars. He was wearing United States military utilities, flak jacket, and a helmet that he had removed from a dead Marine. All I had to defend myself with was my pistol, not an accurate weapon except in close range. I knew if I missed my shot or wounded him, he would empty his thirty-round clip into me. I attempted to alert my buddies, but each one was looking in a different direction as they tried to cover our position. As he moved closer, I knew I had to make the first move, but before I could, he saw me and pointed his rifle. I yelled for help from my friend Ronnie Fields who was across the trail as I shot and wounded the approaching NVA. Fields dived out onto the trail, rolling and screaming like a crazy Marine with his rifle blazing in the direction of the NVA soldier. Bullets flew everywhere from my pistol, Field's rifle, and the NVA's AK-47. Finally, the NVA was down and we were still alive. Fields was hit in his left knee and right arm, but he was still able to fight. I felt awful that Ronnie had just taken two bullets for me, but I was grateful we were both alive. Ronnie deserved a medal for his act of bravery in saving my life and the lives of the other Marines huddled in that small group.[5]

Our position had now been identified, and we were drawing small arms fire and mortars again. I turned around just in time to see an NVA throw a grenade at me. I covered my face as I dived into the dirt. The grenade exploded in the air overhead; the shrapnel penetrated both my ears and burned like fire. My ears were ringing so loud I thought I would lose consciousness. I was temporarily deaf, but again I was alive and thankful, knowing that God was protecting me. Another Marine cut down the NVA with his rifle.

Before I left for Vietnam, some people said to me, "I could never shoot or kill another person." I know how they felt, but let me explain something. If you are looking down the barrel of an AK-47 and the enemy is trying to kill you, you will think differently. In my mind, there is no question what you will do. It is a natural instinct to do whatever you must do to protect yourself and your friends.

The ground began to burn around us from the explosions. The enemy was using flame-throwers to set the dry elephant grass and brush on fire on both sides of our positions. They were trying to flush us out into the open, and it worked. When Marines ran out from the burning grass, they were shot. We were in a spot with intense heat and knew we had to move. We were assisting the wounded and trying to move further back through the burning brush and elephant grass. As I moved, I found a fellow Marine who had been shot in the hip and needed help. I grabbed him and began moving him back when another barrage of mortar rounds landed, throwing hot metal everywhere. The two of us had no place to go, so we just hugged each other and the ground. Another mortar round hit

---

[5] American politicians and the press had been saying that we should not take any action that would involve China or Russia and possibly bring them into the war. But after seeing the size of this gook (enemy soldier), I figured China was already involved.

close by and exploded, throwing hot, jagged shrapnel all around us. I felt excruciating pain and burning in my left arm, and I knew I had been hit. I was afraid to look, fearing I had lost my arm. I glanced at my arm and was overcome with relief to see it was still there. I managed to remove part of the shrapnel, but three pieces were deep in my arm and have remained there for the rest of my life.

At the Marine Command Post at Con Thien, Lieutenant Colonel Schening had heard about our fight and was encouraging Captain Coates through intermittent radio contact to hold his position because help was on the way. It was obvious that Bravo Company was outnumbered by the NVA and might lose this battle if reinforcements did not come quickly. Schening directed Alpha Company to move over land to us and ordered Charley Company at Dong Ha to helicopter onto the strip. He also directed Delta Company at Con Thien to organize a tank infantry relief force. Schening's desire was to be with his Marines in the field, but his orders were to hold Con Thien and the DMZ. He would have been in violation of his primary mission if he abandoned Con Thien, so his only option was to direct the battle from this post. It was impossible for him to calculate whether Bravo Company had encountered an NVA Company, battalion, or regiment, but he knew that we were in serious trouble. If Bravo Company was not able to hold on, then waves of NVA would break through the wire at Con Thien.

In my distress I cried to the Lord, and He heard me. (Psalm 20:1 NIV)

We had been overrun by the NVA, and our company was in ragged pieces. Outnumbered, all we could hope to do was protect each other and try to stay alive. The enemy was well equipped with AK-47s, artillery, CS gas, and 82mm mortars. They had rocket launchers, some flame-throwers, and plenty of ammo. Most of the gas they attempted to spray on us was caught by the wind and blown back on them. The NVA soldiers were wearing Marine Corps helmets and clothing, making it difficult to recognize the enemy. The fighting was close and intense. We lost many good Marines and witnessed many heroic acts. Staff Sergeant Burns attacked and killed an NVA soldier carrying a flame thrower, shooting him four times with his 12-gauge shotgun. With only his bayonet, Private first class

Zimberlin chased down and killed an enemy soldier carrying a machine gun. He was then shot and killed by enemy soldiers. Many of the Marines continued to fight after being wounded multiple times as they helped each other load their rifles. I am amazed and proud of the way our Marines fought and died helping each other. They were true heroes.

Relief finally arrived in the form of F4B Phantom II jets and UH1E Huey gunships, along with the help of the prop-driven 01E Bird Dog observation plane. The Bird Dog dropped white phosphorus rockets to mark targets for the Phantom jets as they dropped their 250-and 500-pound bombs. The Hueys, with their M60 machine guns, were blazing as they pursued the NVA. The air strikes were called in by 1st Platoon SSgt Leon R. "Lee" Burns, who received a Bronze Star for his actions during the Hill Fights at Khe Sanh. He also received a Navy Cross and a meritorious promotion to gunnery sergeant for his bravery during Operation Buffalo. Thankfully, he was not wounded during his tour in Vietnam. After all of our officers were killed, Sergeant Burns took charge of our company. A man highly respected by Marines, he is the perfect example of a Marine who is willing to give his life for others. Many of us owe our lives to him.

As I looked up and saw the jets coming, they seemed to be only a hundred feet above us. I could see the pilot and thought he gave me the thumbs up. We could see stabilizers open up for the bombs as they were released close to us. The impact bounced us around on the ground and covered us with clods of dirt and debris from the blast. We felt like we were being bombed, but we were happy to have some relief.

Napalm bombs were dropped amid the deafening blur of jets just feet above us and into the NVA positions. Napalm is a gelled gasoline which burns at temperatures of 800 to 1200 degrees Celsius, rapidly deoxygenating the available air and creating large amounts of carbon monoxide. When the burning gel gets on your skin, it cannot be extinguished, but has to burn up the gel along with human flesh before it goes out. The bombs were so close to us that the burning gas sucked the oxygen right out of the air, making it difficult to breathe. I felt my chest would explode. We were afraid we would die from the napalm because we could barely breathe and were about to pass out. The black-laced flames and balls of fire seemed to engulf everything around us, but I am not aware of any Marines who died that day because of the napalm gas.

Our Phantom jets had the NVA on the run, but the enemy still managed to shoot down a couple of our planes. Captain Pendagraft's Phantom crashed into the South China Sea, killing him and his co-pilot. Another F8 Crusader also went down, but the pilot, Captain Martin, managed to parachute out and was rescued from the sea by an Air Force helicopter.

A tank had intentionally rolled over my mortar, destroying it from further use by the enemy. We inched our way back along the trail, trying to regroup. We found our other mortar; I quickly disassembled it and gave it to Lance Corporal Cull to carry out. We were battle weary but continued working to regroup. The NVA kept coming, firing small arms, throwing grenades, and dropping mortar rounds on our position. They crossed the intersection of Route 561 in full force, screaming and shooting at everyone in sight.

The NVA were professional killers, trained to fight to the finish. They gave our group of outnumbered Marines a real fight. In a one-on-one fight, the enemy could not compete against Marines, but with these odds, they were winning the battle. The few men from Bravo Company still able to fight were meeting the enemy head on in what was some of the most vicious fighting of the Vietnam War. Already wounded, Corporal Garza continued firing his M60 machine gun into the advancing enemy line, killing multiple soldiers before he was killed. The last radio transmission from Bravo Platoons Two and Three came from Captain Keneipp, a short-timer due to transfer home in just a few days. He sent a message to the Battalion Command Post (CP) at Con Thien, saying, "We are being overrun and will not be talking to you again." As he hung up the radio phone, Captain Keneipp was killed, along with Company Commander Captain Coates, Lieutenant King, Corporal Demers, Corporal Haines, Lance Corporal Bradley, and numerous other Marines.

As we made our way back towards the LZ, half crawling and half running through the burning bushes and tree limbs, we fired our weapons and threw grenades we had taken from dead Marines. Still carrying my .45 pistol, I was desperately searching for an M16 rifle that worked. I saw rifles lying everywhere beside dead Marines, but every one that I picked up was jammed. It was sad to think how many Marines were lost because their rifle malfunctioned.[6]

The bodies of dead and mangled Marines, as well as NVA, were scattered everywhere. We searched for wounded Marines, patched them up with our first aid kits, and then carried them out with us. Many were severely wounded and died as we made our way back. I noticed a Marine crying as he talked to his dead buddy on the ground, desperately trying to get him up and make him move. I grabbed the Marine and shook him, trying to convince him that his buddy was dead and he had to move on. It was difficult to leave them, but we had no choice.

As we moved along the trail, we looked for the wounded among the dead and helped them to the Medevac helicopters at the LZ. Suddenly we were attacked by 60-caliber machine gun fire from the brush. I was caught in the middle of the trail as the machine gun tore up the ground, headed straight for me. I had no place to go, so I dived into the burning bushes to escape the gun fire. Other Marines were not so lucky. One Marine was hit in the stomach and crawled into a bomb crater while continuing to fire back at the machine gun position. We knocked out the machine gun, but the severely wounded Marine was in bad shape. He managed to patch himself up using his field dressing, but in a few minutes he was dead.

Our situation seemed hopeless until I heard the most beautiful sound on earth, the creaking of the tanks coming to our rescue. The tanks, led by 1st Lt. Gatlin Howell, came storming in, firing and making an opening for us. Lieutenant Howell had been Bravo's 3rd Platoon commander for more than eight months and had earned the respect of all the Marines. My first encounter with him came on my first Vietnam patrol in the field. It was late in the day, and we had stopped for a short break. I was hot and tired when I spotted a tree stump that looked like a comfortable place to sit and rest. I sat down and pulled out my canteen for a drink of water. Howell came over to me and said, "Marine, did you check that stump for booby traps?" I replied "No, Sir." Then he said, "You are going to die over here." Those sobering words were my reminder to stay alert and cautious

---

6 I was wishing that the battle-proven M-14 rifles had not been replaced with the non-effective, prone-to-jamming, and low-energy-impacting, plastic weapon known as the M-16. The M-16 was designed by Eugene Morrison Stoner and in my opinion, was pushed into service by United States Secretary of Defense Robert McNamara before it was battle proven.

about everything I did. Lieutenant Howell was a good leader who cared about his men. He had been pulled out of the field and was serving as the battalion intelligence officer, but he was concerned about Bravo Company. Even though his time left in Vietnam was short, he volunteered to come and help us. And help us he did! He saved the lives of the few of us who were left.

Delta Company came to our rescue with the four tanks from Con Thien. The tanks had done a great job of helping us, but two of them were quickly disabled. An enemy RPG-7 Soviet anti-tank gun knocked out one of the tanks. (The RPG-7 is a bazooka-like weapon with projectiles that fly almost 1,000 feet a second and can penetrate eleven inches of steel armor.) Another tank ran over a land mine. It exploded and knocked the tracks off the tank, making it useless. Only two tanks were left in operation.

We were exhausted from being in battle all day in unbearable heat, without food and water, just trying to survive. Charlie Company arrived in helicopters from Dong Ha along with other Marines from the 1st and 3rd Battalion, 9th Marines. They attacked the enemy from their left flank which began to turn the tide of battle. Some of the NVA temporarily retreated to the DMZ, but the fighting continued for another five days.

I finally reached the evacuation area and begin to load the wounded Marines on a Medevac helicopter. We loaded as many wounded on the chopper as it would carry, including Ronnie Fields, who had been shot twice while saving my life. My assistant gunner, Private First Class Weldon, had been shot twice; Private First Class Henderson had five separate wounds. Corporal Trevino had been shot twice, captured, recovered, and then blown off a mined tank and One Marine that had been shot in the hip. We loaded forty seriously wounded Marines on that chopper.

I must have been a mess because a corpsman at the helicopter looked at me and said, "Wait, Marine! Get on the chopper; you are seriously wounded." I replied, "No," not realizing my face and neck were caked with blood from my bleeding ears, blood was running down my arm from the shrapnel wounds, and my clothes and flak jacket were coated with dirt, sweat, and blood, both mine and from those I had helped. The corpsman wrote down my name, and I later received a Purple Heart medal.[7] I was not awarded the Purple Heart medal in the usual awards ceremony, but I did receive it in the mail after I was discharged and returned home.

We loaded all the dead Marines we could recover on two tanks. It was a gruesome task and something I will never forget. They were our dead buddies, our friends, whose charred bodies bore open wounds from shrapnel and gun shots. Many were without body parts; hands, arms, feet, legs, and heads were missing. The worst part was seeing Marines who had been mutilated by the NVA. We had to heave the bodies onto the tanks and stack them like sardines. A while later, Gunny Burns sent word for any Marine left from Bravo and Delta Company to mount the tanks with our KIAs (Killed in Action) and return to Con Thien. The road back to Con Thien was bumpy and dusty, and we kept busy trying to keep our dead Marines from falling off the tanks.

We had killed around 275 of the enemy, but our companies had been destroyed as a fighting unit, with ninety-five dead and over two hundred wounded. We had fifty-nine Marines and corpsmen KIA and more than sixty wounded and evacuated from Bravo Company alone on that 2nd day of July. The stats later revealed that the NVA had unleashed over a thousand artillery and mortar rounds on the Gio Linh and Con Thien areas and seven hundred rounds of that ammunition had fallen on the 1/9 Marines. The mixed smell of charred bodies, burned vegetation, acrid aroma of cordite, and burned petroleum was thick in the air and made me sick to my stomach. This battle was not only called "Operation Buffalo," but also came to be called "The Marketplace Massacre of Bravo Company." It was the worst single disaster of a Marine Corps rifle company during the entire Vietnam War.[8]

There were many heroes that day. Most of our Marines did not get medals or recognition for deeds above and beyond the call of duty. We did what we had to do and what was expected of a United States Marine. Why did my fellow Marines die on this battlefield?

---

[7] The Purple Heart is a United States military decoration awarded in the name of the President to those wounded or killed, while serving, on or after April 5, 1917, with the U.S. military. The Purple Heart is the oldest military award still given to U.S. military members. From Wikipedia, the free encyclopedia

[8] At the end of Operation Buffalo on July 14th there were reported enemy losses of 1,290 dead and two captured with no reports of the wounded NVA. We had losses of 159 Marines killed and 345 wounded.

They died to protect their fellow Marines; to stop the spread of communism from North Vietnam, Russia, and China; and to preserve the right to freedom in South Vietnam and America.

Because the fighting was not over, three more days passed before the rest of our dead Marines could be retrieved. Many of them had not only been killed but also mutilated by the NVA in horrific ways. Many were shot and stabbed multiple times; some had been nailed to trees and stripped of tattoos and body parts. It is hard to believe that men can be so cruel to other men. Again, we were the walking dead, more dead than alive. Seeing our buddies die these horrible deaths left us with awful mental scars that have haunted us for the rest of our lives. What was left of Bravo Company finally made it back to Con Thien, where our wounds were treated. We tried to get our minds back on the task at hand. We felt guilty to have reinforcement Marines still battling the NVA. Many Marines were in shock, like my good friend LCorp Simon Cull, who was later evacuated for a few days and then returned to our company. Most of us had that famous "thousand yard stare" that Marines have after seeing too much combat, witnessing the dead and dying, and seeing our mutilated Marine brothers. We had been touched by death's embrace like never before. We were in a little safer place, but we still had our battle positions to maintain at Con Thien and the bombings just would not stop. We took our positions on the south wall of Con Thien, assigned by Staff Sergeant Burns. We felt numb, wounded inside, and exhausted, but we busied ourselves cleaning our weapons and sharpening our bayonets. I don't think we could have stayed awake had it not been for the continuous explosions from rockets and mortars and the flashbacks from all that we had just been through. I prayed for my fallen comrades and for the Marines of 1/9, 2/9 and 3/9 who continued battling in the hot spot by the DMZ and the Market Place. I was very thankful to God that I was alive and in one piece. Most of us had been wounded, but we were fortunate just to be alive. I waited until morning to get my wounds cleaned and patched because many Marines were in more serious condition. The next morning (July 3rd), shortly after daylight, the call came in for a work party. With so few of Bravo Company left, (only twenty-six), the selection process was abbreviated. We had thirty to forty KIAs laid out on the LZ at Con Thien that needed to be loaded on choppers. Sgt. Richard Huff told us what was going on and what we had to do. Someone asked, "There's an artillery battery, most of H&S (Headquarters and Service), and some more grunts, so why do we have to do it?" Huff's reply was very calm. In a fatherly fashion, he replied, "Guys, I understand this is about as bad a job as there is, but those are our Marine brothers, and we take care of our own." To me that showed Huff's character. Dave Granger commented later, "I've never felt as bad as I did that morning, but Sergeant Huff's wisdom and understanding got me through it."

LETTERS AND COMMENTS FROM OTHER MARINES ABOUT OPERATION BUFFALO

Corporal Tim Haley Section leader 60mm Mortars of Charlie Company 1st Battalion 9th Marines

"On July 2nd, we were in Dong Ha when we were alerted that Bravo Company was in deep trouble. They had walked right into a huge regimental size NVA ambush. We were told to saddle up and get back to the DMZ to reinforce Bravo Company. We loaded on helicopters and headed back for the DMZ where Bravo had just relieved us a few days earlier. Flying into the Landing Zone we could see incoming enemy mortars, artillery and rockets exploding everywhere and we were flying into this maelstrom. After getting hit by shrapnel and getting shot at by unfriendly NVA soldiers, I worked my way to a group of Marines in a hand grenade duel with the NVA and, upon looking east towards the ocean as we entered onto a trail I saw a group of a dozen or so Marines, tattered and torn, bloody and dirty with the look of terror and exhaustion. At this moment, I recognized "POPS," Derl Horn. We called him that because he was married and a few years older than us 18 year olds. Derl and I had been through boot camp, ITR training, 81mm mortar training, Camp Lejuene and Cuba together. We were sent to Vietnam at the same time and both ended up in 1/9 with the 3rd Marine Division but in different companies; he went to Bravo and I went to Charlie

Company. Out of the whole company of Marines in Bravo these seem to be all of the survivors. There actually ended up being a total of 26. The fight went on for several more days but what Bravo suffered was the worst and was known from then on as "July 2nd" the day Bravo Company was wiped out. I personally saw mutilated Marines and Corpsmen, the NVA had abused and killed over 100 Marines on the 2nd. The NVA had gone through the kill zone and shot the wounded in the head. We then worked our way west towards Con Thien and help set up a medevac Landing Zone. I lost contact with Derl after this fight and hoped he had gotten out of there alive."

Lance Corporal Simon Cull a Gunner with 60mm Mortars in Bravo Company 1st Battalion 9th Marines

"Since that long battle on July 2nd when you, Derl Horn was wounded and I was medevac'd I often wonder if you go through the flash backs of that Vietnam War that I go through. I find it hard to forget July 2nd, 1967 of Operation Buffalo when you and I and 24 other Marines survived out of the whole Bravo Company. That deadly day has affected my life. I am happy that you survived as well as Tom Hines, Ronnie Fields, Richard Huff and Gunny Burns. I guess you can say that I am one of those shell shocked Marines."

PFC Dave Granger of 1st Platoon in Bravo Company 1st Battalion 9th Marines

"On July 2nd, 1st Platoon stayed back while the rest of our company moved north up the main road. We were to load the water cans from yesterday's resupply on choppers that was bringing in more ammo. It was not long after the rest of our company moved out and we had finished with the water cans that we heard a firefight break out up the road. We dropped everything, grabbed the M60 ammo and took off up the trail. We did not have to go all the way to where the lead platoon was in order to be caught up in the ambush. The more we fired the more of them began moving. After a while it was like we had kicked an ant bed. They were everywhere, in close with more coming in the distance. We quickly began taking casualties and that limited any major movements. We were basically pinned down in place. Ammo started getting low and our M16's began malfunctioning. Those of us still able to move began taking weapons and ammo off the dead and dying and passing it to anyone still able to shoot."

Lance Corporal Roger Good an M79 man from 3rd Platoon Delta Company 1st Battalion 9th Marines

"The morning of July 2nd, I was given supply duty and took a mule (a small motor vehicle) to the far side of Con Thien to pick up C-rations when someone from 3rd Platoon Delta came running over to tell me that Bravo was in trouble and we were moving out to help them. I raced over the hill and found the four tanks that were already assembled and ready to go, so I grabbed my M-79, two satchels with bags full of M79 rounds and my .45 pistol and climbed on a tank. There may have been 12 to 15 of us on the tanks along with a jeep with Captain Radcliffe, Lt. Howell and Radioman Thompson. We went hell bent for leather down the hill on the north side and turned left across the clearing into the jaws of hell. The battle was engaged as we hit the north end of the trace. Our tanks were firing all weapons and we dismounted, some were directed to take up a position around the edge of the clearing and Lance Corporal Ron Potter and I continued North with one tank and the officers. We set up our position about 200 meters on the northern leg of the perimeter near the Marketplace, just the two of us. The firefight was ongoing and we could hear the NVA talking as they continued to probe our position, not knowing there were only two of us which they could have over run. The incoming was relentless and we knew that we were in big trouble. I remember chambering a beehive round I had acquired and sat back for an instant and made my peace with the Lord but vowed to take a bunch of the NVA with me on my last shot. About that time an F4 came directly over us at about 100 feet and began dropping his bombs right at us because the

NVA were so close. We got to the bottom of our holes and could hear and feel debris all over us from the explosions. The impact lifted me out of my hole and slammed me back into it. I heard Potter yelling, asking if I was ok and I responded "yes" and stood up but fell back. My legs would not work due to my head being screwed up from the blast. Potter grabbed me and headed south toward the firebreak. Rounds were thick as hornets. Potter dropped me once to engage the gooks that were close behind us then grabbed me again to help me to the edge of the trace. Choppers were coming in with Charlie Company out of Dong Ha and landing on the LZ but before Potter could get me there they took off again because of artillery and mortars zeroing in on the LZ. Potter managed to get me to a corpsman already tending to wounded Marines, one of them with his leg blown off above his knee. The femoral artery was squirting blood about three feet with each heart beat. I could hear the Marine praying The Lord's Prayer and we all joined in. The shells kept exploding and we kept praying—*"give us this day our daily bread and forgive us our trespasses as we forgive those who trespass against us, and lead us not into temptation but deliver us from evil."* As we prayed and the wounded Marine said "Amen," the stream of blood stopped and he died. I don't remember anything after that until I woke up in a panic. I couldn't move and the smell of death was everywhere. Something was on me and I could not move but could hear voices and realized that I needed help so I forced my arm out and started yelling. Someone heard me and pulled me out from under the heap of dead bodies that had been loaded on tanks. I was taken into the medical bunker on Con Thien where I was examined and patched up and told to sit in the corner until I could be observed. I watched the wounded and dying being tended to until I could not watch anymore and that is when I returned to my position. It was dark and my day was over."

Blood, Sweat and Honor

Private First Class Steve Weldon of
Bravo Company 2nd Platoon 1st Battalion 9th Marines

"I lost contact with everyone in my squad so I was making my way through the brush west of Route 561 searching for friends and ran onto two Marines from 1st Platoon in a ditch. The NVA started shooting at us from our rear and up front and to our left so we opened fire in all directions. One of our Marines' M16 jammed and I had a ramrod that I gave him. I turned back just as I was shot with a burst from an AK47, which knocked me down. There I was, in shock, on my back with half of my left biceps gone. I was in an odd position but managed to get my M16 back just as an NVA walked up looking at me and laughed. I managed to blow him away with a burst from my M16. I then realized that my two Marine buddies were dead. I was alone again and not in very good shape so I started crawling through the brush and running through the open areas. Suddenly I felt a sharp pain when a bullet tore a crease across my butt. Finally, I made it to a crater marked by a small-uprooted banana tree. I sat in the dirt to stop the bleeding in my butt. I almost shot one of our attached Company engineers as he jumped in the crater with me. I was feeling weak from blood loss so the engineer helped to bandage my wounds. With the Engineers help we found other Marines to be with as the mortar rounds were falling all around us. We were getting some help from air strikes then and realized just how close they were when we could read the numbers on the Phantoms as they came over, dropping their 250 to 500 lb. bombs. I was calling for a Corpsman, thinking I was going to bleed to death but there were no Corpsmen. My engineer buddy helped get me back to several Marines huddled in a bomb crater. I seemed to be fading in and out of consciousness as I lay in the crater. We managed to make it to the LZ (Landing Zone) and I was helped on the Sea Knights helicopter to be lifted away to safety. I was weak and bleeding from my two gunshot wounds but now I was away from the fight. I am happy to say that I survived and would be discharged from the Marine Corps in two years as a Corporal with 30% disability."

DERL HORN

Lance Corporal Ray Linebaugh, Alpha Company, 2nd Platoon 1st Battalion, 9th Marines

"Alpha Company, First Battalion 9th Marines was on a brief stand down at Dong Ha, a well deserved rest. It was June the 26th my birthday, I remember drinking beer and eating hot chow and sleeping, but the stand down was short lived. June 30th 1967, we were back in the field, north east of Con Thien. Bravo Company was already there just east of our position; our mission was to sweep the area north of the trace, reporting any enemy movement. The area was full of rice patties, waste high grass with bomb craters and old vacant villages. The temperature was extremely hot. July the 1st our company went north east toward Bravo. The heat was a factor for new guys, when the choppers came in bringing drinking water and sea rations at the end of the day, a heat stroke Marine victim was air lifted out.

Bravo Company was 1500 meters east when we set camp. It was dark and we were told to be ready for anything. My squad was sent out for a night patrol. I was outside the perimeter no more than twenty feet when word came from the front that our point man had bumped into an NVA, they both backed away without incident. We were told to sit down right where we were and stay put until morning.

The morning of July 2nd we heard small arms fire and mortars dropping from Bravo Company's position. The fire fight got more intense as we worked our way toward them, then all hell broke loose. We began to get incoming mortars, wounding several. We continued and our point man tripped a mine wounding several. Captain Slater had Lieutenant Muller, 3rd platoon leader, establish a medevac LZ. He was to hold the LZ perimeter until all wounded Marines were out of the field.

Captain Slater sent 1st platoon Staff Sergeant Leslie to drive north and then east to establish contact with Bravo Company. Captain Slater took 2nd platoon, which I was part of, due east to establish contact with Bravo Company. On our way it rained mortars on our advance. The NVA had turned their attack on us. I was in a ditch with three Marines as the mortars hit on all sides. The NVA had a habit of walking- in their mortars. I looked up and sixty feet in front of me was an NVA wearing a flak jacket and a helmet carrying an M16. I knew it was a gook, but I hesitated, it was hard to shoot that Marine uniform, I thought" what if I'm wrong?" I asked the radio man with me to find out if Charley Company was in the area. I knew they had to be on their way. About that time, a gook in full NVA gear stepped out to greet the man in the marine gear. I waved, he waved and I shot both of them. It was still very hard to shoot our uniform. Another volley of mortars hit close to our ditch, a Marine named Horace started to run and I grabbed him and pulled him down, yelling for him to "Stay put!." Another round hit closer, Horace bolted from the hole and was hit by another mortar. The Corpsman with me started to run to his aid, I pulled him back and told him," there is nothing he can do for Horace, stay put." When I turned around, the Corpsman jumped out to aid Horace. A mortar round landed near them, killing the Corpsman. Suddenly it began raining mortars, one hit so close to our hole I was knocked unconscious, as I came to, I felt numb from head to toe, my hearing came back slowly, and although covered with dirt we were not seriously injured.

Captain Slater got word that Alpha Company's, 3rd platoon was now being overrun. 3rd platoon had secured a perimeter for medevac choppers and then was to join 2nd platoon to make our way to Bravo Company, which now was fully engaged with the full initial force of an NVA attack. Slater turned 2nd platoon back around to try to rescue 3rd platoon, which was under a heavy ground attack.

Lieutenant Muller, who was in charge of 3rd platoon, was mortally wounded by the time 2nd platoon turned around to help them. Second platoon was hit hard by snipers and stopped in a rice patty with a border hedgerow. They soon became overwhelmed by the NVA forces, that had been attacking 3rd platoon. Slater had us make a perimeter in the rice patty, and we could see remnants of 3rd platoon, some wounded, bodies strewn all around us.

I told Captain Slater, who was on one knee with the radio calling in air strikes, he had better get down because a lot of fire power was coming through the hedgerow. He bent down, trying to seek cover but still continued to call in air strikes. Most of our men were suffering from lack of water, were low on ammunition, and feeling the pains of exhaustion. We took turns running out from our positions and grabbing Marines and pulling them into our perimeter, all the while being shot at by snipers. We grabbed a big Marine, who was lifeless. It was Lieutenant Muller; he had leg wounds, but was stone cold dead.

We went back to grab a tall, lifeless machine gunner named Ragland. When we went to grab him, he opened his eyes, saw it was us, and ran back with us inside the hedgerow while being shot at. He was laughing and crying at the same time! He told us that he had played dead while his two gunner assistants on either side of him were killed. He said the worst part was that they drank his water and stuck a bayonet beside his head to see if he would move. They did this over and over again as the NVA soldiers came through. This rescue experience was one of the best things that happened that day.

Towards the end of the day, Captain Slater had us fix bayonets, telling us to get ready to defend ourselves. The heat and lack of water was almost more than we could stand. When we didn't think it could get any worse, IT DID! The NVA started burning the hedge rows. The smoke was bad, and I began to realize that this could be the end. Captain Slater called in airstrikes so close the concussion lifted me off the ground and the attack on us seemed to stop.

A Marine came busting through our perimeter. He asked, "Is this Alpha Company?" Slater said, "Yes, what's left of it." He said, "I'm with 3/9 and we have clear passage back to the strip." Charlie Company had made it and they were there helping rescue Bravo. Now, Charlie Company was taking the brunt with casualties but saved many who would not have made it out. I later found out that 1st platoon was ambushed and pinned down on their way to help Bravo company. Toward the end of the day, they made it and helped recover the dead and wounded.

After our rescue, I seen the bodies of Bravo Company Marines being carried out in poncho litters, I was devastated to see so many KIA's, I thank God for all those who did survive. For that reason this was the best day and the worse day of my life."

E-5 Phil Sutherland, Gun section leader of the 106mm recoilless rifle platoon company with H&S Company 1/9 at Con Thien, attached to Bravo Company

"I remembered watching Bravo Company leave Con Thien on June 30th heading out towards the DMZ and wondered how they would fare with a brand new in-country commander. Captain Coates had just been assigned to Bravo and this was his first day taking over the company. Captain Coates was from my home town in Pennsylvania. A couple of days later on July 2nd, we could see and hear explosions going off in the distance with a large amount of gunfire. We were told that Bravo Company was pinned down out in the Trace and that they had run into a much bigger force of at least two NVA Battalions. I cannot give you the perspective of actually being in the battle, although it was my desire at the time to do so. We were volunteering to go out and help Bravo but were instructed to man the perimeter in anticipation that Con Thien could be attacked. Bravo finally got some relief with the help of other Battalion companies, tanks and Phantom jets dropping bombs and napalm. From July 2nd through July 13th, the NVA retaliated by dropping around 350 rounds per day from mortars, rockets and artillery on Con Thien and the surrounding areas. This was one of the most costly battles during Vietnam. I still can picture it in my mind to this day."

Lance Corporal Mike Hogan a fire team Leader in 2nd squad of 2nd platoon assigned to Hotel 2/9

"On July 2nd, 1967, my Company was on the south side of Con Thien taking in some mortar rounds but the north side was being bombarded. We then heard that Bravo 1/9 had been overrun and that we were to be helicoptered in to help out. We were told to carry as much ammo and water as we could. I had only been in country about a month and although I had been in a couple of fire fights, I had never been told to carry all the ammo that you possibly can. This coupled with the fact that all of the guys who had been in Nam for awhile were talking about how bad this was going to be scared the crap out of me. We boarded helicopters, were taken a short distance and landed under heavy fire on the strip close to a smoldering helicopter. We were told to find cover because there were NVA everywhere. My position was close to the LZ so every time a chopper even came close to landing the gooks would open up with mortar and artillery rounds along with automatic weapons.

The NVA were walking the mortar rounds toward our position so we moved north towards the edge of the strip. We were told that the main trail being used by 1/9 was in front of us and to only fire when we could be sure that it was the enemy. This was difficult because some of the enemy were wearing Marine utilities and helmets taken from dead Marines. Choppers were trying to bring in supplies and ammo but could not land so they were dropping supplies as close as they could from the air. The only time they were landing was to pick up wounded Marines. During one of these landings, with mortar rounds hitting everywhere a piece of shrapnel tore through my right thigh pocket and hit my fully loaded magazine. It was hot and jagged but did not penetrate my body. Later on July 29th, I realized how lucky I was after being wounded twice during an intense battle with the NVA. I still carry two pieces of shrapnel in my upper right chest.

The NVA began some intense automatic weapons fire to the point we thought they were going to charge us. I noticed a female gook running from my left to my right fifty yards or so in front of me; she was dressed in the traditional black pants and long white top and hat. She was carrying a long pole with a basket on each end of the pole. I remember thinking that the way that pole was bent that she must be carrying something heavy. About the time I realized that it was probably ammo, she disappeared into the brush. To this day I still have night mares about her, knowing that I should have shot her. I wonder how many Marines were wounded or killed because I let her get away. Later I saw another female gook running the opposite direction carrying the same kind of load and I did fire two rounds at her.

As I was looking to the north I saw a Marine calmly walking down the trail towards my position with the enemy firing the whole time. As this Marine got closer, I realize that I knew him and that we had been in boot camp and ITR together. I yelled, "Garcia, get down.

There are gooks all over the place!" He was bloody and dirty and said to me, "This is nothing." He pointed down the trail and said, "They are blowing horns and yelling at us." I asked him what he was doing and he replied, "Looking for ammo because everyone is out." As he was picking up ammo and headed back down the trail he turned and said, "Keep your head down, Hogan." To this day I do not know if he made it out or not.

Choppers started landing again bringing in new Marines. These Marines were real new still in their state side utilities and boots. As the fighting had subsided, I could still see Marines carrying out the dead and wounded past my position. Some of those state side boots could be seen on the dead Marines as they stacked the bodies at the LZ. I still am plagued with flashbacks from that day.

Although my MOS was 0341 Mortars, I was always assigned to a rifle squad and eventually made a squad leader. I was honorably discharged as a corporal in December, 1968.

Hospital Corpsman Jon Vandercook
Bravo 1st Battalion 9th Marines

I was restricted to Con Thien on a medical hold from an Orthopedist at Delta Med in Dong Ha; my desire was to be with Bravo Company. I had spent several days with a platoon from Delta Company on the perimeter at Con Thien. Bravo Company was already north of Con Thien. Word came down that part of Delta was moving out into the field. Since I couldn't go out to the field, I was relieved by HN Phillip Converse who would later be killed in my place. I really couldn't tell him much about the platoon since I had been temporarily assigned for a short period of time. I went back to the Battalion Aid station bunker on top of the hill. Late that afternoon Major Danielson, 1/9's Executive Officer, was ordered to take the available vehicles out on the strip to pick up Bravo Company survivors. HM3 Ron Coffman and I left the Battalion aid station and went with the three vehicle convoy to pick up Bravo survivors. We treated the wounded survivors and after loading the wounded onto the vehicle the convoy departed to return to Con Thien. Enemy artillery incoming halted the convoy so the wounded were unloaded and when the artillery stopped, we reloaded and returned to Con Thien. The next morning we had to identify and tag the KIA (Killed in Action) Marines that were brought back."

Sergeant C.B. Clement with S-4 crew

"While at Con Thien during July I was with the S-4 crew located just below 81 Mortars on the North side, next to the LZ (landing zone). I was in charge of the Polan 155 Infared sniper night scope battery racks at the generators and repairing or replacing weapons.

On July 2nd, we all knew what was happening to Bravo and that they were in big trouble with the NVA. We had our own battle at Hill of Angels for four days with gook artillery hitting us constantly with their 60mm and 82mm mortars from all sides and their 152mm long range guns from the DMZ 6 miles away. On July 6th, the shelling had not stopped. It seemed like it was raining steel from one large continuous explosion. We had an ambulance jeep trying to make it up the hill when it was hit by a rocket knocking out the engine and wounding the driver and passengers. We ran out to help them in between mortar explosions, using a stretcher. We made it back to our position with the wounded. I then discovered that I was covered with blood. I thought it was from the wounded but it was from the piece of shrapnel stuck in my left temple. The next day I was on my way to Dong Ha to have my wounds treated. I looked back just in time to see a 152mm delayed round hit our command bunker taking out the **whole 1/9 command center."**

Picture Derl carried with him in Vietnam

14

ALARMING LETTER HOME

On the morning of July 3rd my heart was heavy, but I felt a pressing urgency to write Marilyn a letter. I hoped to reassure her that I was okay. I had to borrow writing gear since I had lost everything in my pack, except my pistol, on the battlefield. It was important to explain about the fierce battle and to let her know that I had been wounded, but not seriously. I didn't want her to worry. I knew she would learn of the battle because she and her parents watched the morning and evening news with Walter Cronkite and read the newspaper daily. She would recognize the name of my division, battalion, and company and would know I was involved in this major battle. I didn't want her to live in fear, not knowing if I was dead or alive until she received my letter in about ten days. Hopefully my letter would give her comfort, knowing I was alive and okay.

■■

July 3, 1967
Dearest Marilyn,

I hardly know how to begin this letter. First of all I want to tell you that I am fine and for you not to worry. Yesterday was a day and a half for me. My company, Bravo, was on the search and destroy sweep that I have been telling you about. We spent the night on the north side of the strip. As we continued on with our mission the morning of July 2nd, things really began to happen. We were ambushed by 4,000 of the North Vietnam Army; this count is not confirmed yet. We were later reinforced by other 1/9 companies. The battle raged all day until we were able to pull out our dead and wounded. I won't lie to you; we have many casualties. We lost a lot of good men, including our Company Commander. Everybody in my mortar section made it out alive but most of us were wounded. I caught mortar shrapnel in my left arm and grenade shrapnel in my ears. It is nothing serious. Please don't let yourself get upset, just take care of yourself and our baby inside you. I hope you get this letter before you hear from anybody else. You will probably get a letter notifying you that I have been wounded because they took my name. My wounds are light compared to most. I had to leave my pack behind with all my letters, pictures, film, Bible etc. and I am sure the enemy got it, so if you should get any fictitious letters telling you that I have been killed or captured, don't believe anything you hear unless it is from me. If something like this should happen, contact the Red Cross to check it out. I will let you know more later, but for now do not believe what you hear from TV or anywhere. You can be proud of your husband; we fought a good fight and I earned a Purple Heart.

I am back at Con Thien again and think I will be going back to Dong Ha soon. Honey, just know that I am fine and if you do not hear from me like you should, it is because of my location and me having to borrow writing gear. Honey, I love you with all my heart. You will always be the most precious thing to me in the whole world. I miss you more each day and am still hoping the time will go fast so I can hurry home to you and our little one. Take care of yourself and don't worry about me and stay mine.
I love you,
Derl

P.S. I am sending you a government check for $164.00 and a $20.00 bill.

Marilyn: On July 2, 1967 Derl's mom, Nellie Horn, and I left early in the morning for my grandmother's home where we had stored all our household items while I lived with Mother and Dad. With two moves to Camp Lejeune, our boxes needed to be organized and marked before Derl returned home. I was too far along in my pregnancy to do it alone. We took a lunch break at noon and to our surprise, my friends Sharon and Dee Spann dropped by for a visit. It was out of the ordinary for them to visit me in the middle of the day, but of course, I didn't know they had seen the morning news about Derl's company and the terrible battle with a large number of casualties. They were concerned about Derl and how I was dealing with the news. When they realized I was not aware of what had happened, they weren't prepared to tell me. Later that evening at work, I picked up the newspaper and began reading the front page. There it was right in front of me: "1st Battalion, 9th Marines, 3rd Marine Division, Bravo Company" and the written description of the horror of what had taken place, including pictures.

It is hard even now to describe the feelings of fear that washed over me. This was Bravo Company, my husband's company! "Oh God, please protect Derl!" I cried. It was impossible to work, so I rushed home to talk with my parents and to call Derl's family.

The next morning we all waited for the morning news segments and the paper. The terrible battle was still raging, making it impossible to recover the bodies of our Marines. All we could do was pray and wait. We had many conversations with Derl's mom and dad, sisters, brother, my family, and friends as we tried to comfort and encourage one another.

I could not sleep. It was hard to turn off my thoughts, yet I knew the baby needed me to rest. I continued asking God to give me faith to trust Him with whatever was ahead for us. During one very difficult night, I was crying out in prayer to the Lord when I felt a calm reassurance that Derl was coming home. I did not hear an audible voice, but in my heart, I knew the Lord was assuring me Derl would come home and we would have a long life together. A deep peace filled my heart, and I thanked the Lord for His reassurance. There were many days ahead when fear would arise in my heart, but I took myself back to that moment when I knew God had assured me of His plan for us. In about six days—a miracle in itself—I received a letter from Derl, written on July 3rd. It was a sweet but sad letter, letting me know he was okay with shrapnel wounds to his ears and left arm, but nothing (he said) to worry about. He was honest and told me many men were wounded and many had died on the battlefield. Those deaths were a struggle and a heartache he would carry for the rest of his life.

About three weeks later, when life was returning to normal, I was home alone when the doorbell rang. I went to the door to find a Western Union man with a telegram in his hand.

I asked, "Who is the telegram for?"

"Marilyn Horn," he answered.

"Who is it from?" I demanded.

He replied, "The Commandant of the Marine Corps."

I felt like my heart had stopped. I remembered hearing about women who had received notice of their husband's death by telegram. Instantly, fear overcame me. I told the young man, "I am here alone so you will have to come back in about thirty minutes when my parents come home for lunch. Then I will sign for the telegram."

"I cannot leave without you signing and taking this telegram," he explained.

I said, "Then, you will just have to wait."

Blood, Sweat and Honor

He sat down on the porch steps and I sat in the kitchen, waiting for my parents. It was a long thirty minutes before they came home. When they arrived, I signed for the letter and he left. We went into the kitchen together where I opened the letter and began reading. When I realized it was telling me about the battle on July 2nd, all three of us were so relieved and thankful for this good news.

Western Union Telegram to Marilyn:
This is to inform you that your husband Lance Corporal H. Derl Horn USMC was injured 2 July 1967 in the vicinity of Quang Tri, Republic of Vietnam. He sustained a fragment wound to the left arm from a mortar round while engaged in action against hostile forces. He was treated in the field and returned to duty. His condition and prognosis were excellent. In view of the above no further reports will be sent to you from this headquarters. His mailing address remains the same. Wallace M Greene Jr., Commandant of the Marine Corps

Marilyn was relieved to know I was alive and had not been wounded again. She and her parents hugged and cried with relief, knowing that I was okay and had not been involved in another battle. This experience was one she would not soon forget.

15

RECUPERATE AND REGROUP

At Con Thien the twenty-six Marines who survived Operation Buffalo began recuperating. Con Thien was not the safest place to recuperate, but it was better than the DMZ. The NVA spent another ten days trying to overrun the base, but thankfully they were unsuccessful. However, they did manage to unleash an ungodly amount of artillery on us. In a few more days thirty new guys were assigned to Bravo Company with the promise of more on the way. Months passed before we were a complete company again. The scary part for us was knowing this would be a new company of men with very little combat experience.

July 4th was a day to celebrate our country's independence, but more exciting to me were the twenty letters I received from home. Many of the letters dated back to May and June, but I didn't care. It was good to have a touch from home. Marilyn was feeling well and getting good reports from her doctor, Dr. James Mashburn. She was still working part time at Heine's Steak House and keeping busy sewing clothes for herself and the baby. There were letters from my parents, Berl and Nellie Horn. I was saddened to learn my loving parents, were getting a divorce after thirty years of marriage. Another letter was from my brother, Berl, who was five years older and living in Michigan. After serving two years in the Army, he had been honorably discharged, then recalled for another year during the Cuban Missile Crisis. At seventeen I felt I should have been called to serve instead of him. I loved my big brother and looked up to him.

There were letters from my two brothers-in-law, Tom Buchanan, still at Camp Pendleton and his brother, Kenneth Buchanan, also a Marine in his fifth week of basic training at MCRD in California. He was eager to come to Vietnam and asked me to save a few VC for him. That didn't appear to be a problem since they seemed to be everywhere we turned. It was good to hear from my sisters Norma Eastburn, who lived in Florida, and Myra DeVault, who lived in Arkansas.

I received letters from many of our friends, including Jim and Joyce Watson, Dee and Sharon Spann, Sam and Jackie Wilson. It was encouraging to know I was loved by my family and friends and they were praying for me. Many of my fellow Marines had come from rough family backgrounds, so I felt fortunate to have a loving and caring family. I felt sorry for Marines who rarely received mail and even sadder for the ones who received "Dear John" letters from their wives or girlfriends.

After many difficult weeks, we had a great day—or at least as good as a day could get at Con Thien. We received new, clean clothes and hot food. I'm not sure how it happened, but we were served roast beef, mashed potatoes, green peas, a slice of pineapple, and cold milk. It was a real treat!

The NVA continued to drop mortars and rockets on Con Thien. We worked hard in between attacks, filling sandbags and ammo boxes with sand and reinforcing our bunkers to be—hopefully—strong enough to take a direct hit. It was unbelievable, as we were bombarded almost hourly throughout the day. On July 7th the enemy dropped a single 152mm shell with a delay-fuse. A direct hit on our well-constructed, 1/9 Command Post bunker at Con Thien, it killed fourteen Marines, including 1st Lt. Gatlin Howell. He was the intelligence officer who came out with tanks to rescue what remained of Bravo Company during the ambush at the DMZ on July 2nd, literally saving our lives.

Among those who died with Howell were two sergeants, four corporals, five lance corporals, and two privates. Ten men survived the blast, but all were badly wounded, including Lt. Col. Richard J. "Spike" Schening. We were devastated. I wondered, *How could the NVA get a lucky shot like that and kill so many good Marines, especially Lieutenant Howell, who had finished his tour and was ready to head home?* In Vietnam, we took one day at a time because we never knew whose name would be on the next mortar, rocket, or sniper fire. Only God knew.

On July 9th we learned from division headquarters that our company, Bravo 1/9, had been recommended for the Presidential Unit Citation, the highest citation given to a combat company. The degree of heroism required is the same as that which warrants awarding of the Distinguished Service Cross to an individual.

Camp Evans

*Robert Brown, Derl Horn, Tom Hines
Simon Cull and Ronnie Fields*

16

OPERATION HICKORY II

After spending twelve days at Con Thien, dodging mortars and rockets, we added seventy-five new Marines to our depleted company, slowly rebuilding Bravo Company. Orders came for us to move to Camp Carroll for our next assignment—Operation Hickory II. Gen William C. Westmoreland, commander of all U.S. forces in South Vietnam, ordered that a sweep be made of the northern area of Quang Tri Province, south of the Ben Hai River. This maneuver was intended to destroy enemy fortifications, mortar and artillery positions in the southern half of the DMZ and to clear concentrations of enemy forces from the southern edge of the DMZ down to the Cam L, Bo Dieu and Cua Viet Rivers. We were headed back into the bush once again.

Our company was transferred to Camp Carroll by truck convoy, not our usual hike through the bush. It would have been a good ride if I could have shaken the fear of our trucks hitting a mine and blowing us into a million pieces. We did our best not to focus on the imminent danger but to enjoy the hot, bumpy, dusty ride. We arrived at Camp Carroll safely and were assigned to sleeping quarters in tents, with cots and an occasional hot meal. These accommodations seemed too good to be true. It felt like heaven to us "Old Salts"[9] after the dusty, dirty bunkers of Con Thien where we had only C-rations

---

[9] "Old Salts" were weathered Marines who were experienced in battle and knew their way around in combat.

to eat. To the new Marines arriving from the US, the camp had miserable accommodations, but to me it was a comfortable place to be. The new guys looked young and inexperienced, including a few cocky "know-it-alls." I knew it would not be long before these self-confident men would be changed by the horror of combat. After only three months in Vietnam, I normally would not have qualified as an "Old Salt," but with the hell I had just been through, I became a member of the league.

While at camp I was able to make one of Marilyn's wishes come true. One Marine had a Polaroid camera, so I asked him to take some pictures to send home. I felt real good after mailing the pictures to her, knowing she would be happy to get them.

***Marilyn:** A few weeks after Derl left for Vietnam, I settled into a rhythm of working, writing letters, and keeping busy with friends, church, sewing, and other hobbies. I worked at distracting myself from thinking about the dangers facing Derl, but it was hard as our family began and ended each day with the TV newscast. The number of dying men was growing, and the thought was not far from my mind that the next casualty could be my husband.*

Each letter Derl sent was an encouragement, and pictures were a special delight. A couple of months after Derl's arrival in Vietnam, he told me he was sending me some pictures. It was hard to wait, but the day finally arrived. I could tell the envelope was heavier than usual, so I quickly opened it. As I looked at the pictures, I was shocked and the tears began to flow. There was Derl's smiling face, but he was so thin I could see his ribs. My fears that he wasn't eating enough were confirmed by these pictures. He had lost a lot of weight. After my initial shock, even though he was thin, I was happy to have a picture and to see his sweet face.

Camp Carroll, one of nine artillery firebases along the DMZ, was equipped with sixteen guns in the center of camp. The eighty-gun artillery fan was completed with the addition of 175mm long-range guns. At Camp Carroll, the Marines could direct artillery fire into almost any grid coordinate from the South China Sea to Laos, as well as into North Vietnam, with help from airfields at Don Ha and Khe Sanh.

The latest rumor around camp was that 1st Battalion 9th Marines would soon be going back to Okinawa, Japan, for more training because of the many new Marines in our outfit. We would have welcomed the training in Okinawa, but there was little hope that it would ever happen. Early on we had been told, "If you do not hear a rumor by noon, go ahead and start one."

We enjoyed the comforts of Camp Carroll for two days when our orders came to head back into the bush. The first day we traveled five miles out from camp and set up our position about a mile from a Vietnamese village inside an old French fort called D-5. This fort was used during the French war from 1945 to 1954. Many people in the States believed we were fighting untrained savages, but in reality, the NVA and VC had defeated the French Foreign Legion years before. During that time, the French Foreign Legion had constructed strong, reinforced underground bunkers made of cement that were still useable. The downside to these old bunkers was that they were damp, moldy, and a haven for rats.

After we arrived, we found one empty bunker with a tin roof and decided to use it for sleeping. We settled in for the night in the old bunker, but, as we drifted off to sleep, we could hear rustling sounds. When someone lit a match, we could see rats running in all directions. We quickly picked up our bedding and crawled out of the bunker to sleep on the ground.

ARVNs (Army of the Republic of Vietnam) used the bunkers for food preparation and sleeping. The food they prepared smelled good and looked appetizing. They had a remarkable ability to find food. They would head into the jungle for a while and return with some type of meat, leaves and vines for a salad, vegetables, and fruits like pineapples, bananas, and limes. The fruit tasted good. On one occasion, I was invited to join them for a meal. I thought it would be better than my daily C-rations. As I watched them clean and prepare the chicken for cooking, my anticipation grew for a tasty, hot meal. Then, to my surprise, they chopped up the internal organs of the chicken they had laid aside while cleaning the chicken and raked them into the pot. It didn't take me long to remember I had a pressing job that needed immediate attention, and I would be unable to join them for dinner. It was C-rations for me.

The daily assignment of guard duty was essential to keep us from being infiltrated by the North Vietnamese. Every day we had sniper fire, and the cement bunkers were good protection from the mortars and rockets. For entertainment from the boredom, we would go into the empty bunkers and chase rats with our bayonets. We did not have many KIA rats.

There was a shortage of .45 pistols for the officers, so I traded mine in for an M-16 rifle. I felt more comfortable with the rifle than the pistol. One mortar, salvaged from the July 2nd ambush, made up our mortar squad. The mortar section worked hard to rebuild one of the damaged bunkers and prepare it to withstand a direct hit from an enemy mortar or rocket round. It was difficult work in the heat and humidity, but it was more important for us to have a safe place for our mortar and our squad.

After three months in the field, I finally received my first pair of jungle boots. Up to that time, I had been wearing regular military boots; one was without a heel, which had come off shortly after arriving in country. I was happy to have a good pair of boots, even though they had been removed from one of our KIA Marines. The jungle boots, lighter than regular military boots, had drain holes in the sides to drain water and mud, allowing our feet to dry. Even with the jungle boots, men experienced "jungle rot" from all the moisture. Any day when we received letters and packages during mail call was a good day. One day I was excited to hear my name called after many days of receiving no mail. I hit the jackpot with thirteen letters, a container of brownies and cookies, and canned goods from home. The brownies and cookies were a bit dry after three weeks in transit, but they still tasted good as I passed the food around to all my buddies. The new guys were disappointed not to have a letter, but they had not been in the country long enough for their mail to catch up with them. I had not forgotten the difficult wait for letters when I first arrived.

As I opened my letters, I was thrilled to find pictures of Marilyn. She looked sweet and beautiful with her little round tummy full of baby. I couldn't wait to show off her pictures to the guys. They acted crazy with cat calls, whistling, and questions about how I was able to get such a beautiful wife. I treasured those pictures from home, but they also made me sad and homesick. I felt so far away, but I wouldn't shed tears or show emotion. I had to protect the image of a tough, mean Marine.

The letters were full of news from home, keeping me connected with family and friends. My mother wrote that she was visiting my brother, Berl, and his family in Michigan. It was a difficult time in our country with race riots taking place across the country. She shared that the family could not get out in the evenings in Muskegon because of the road blocks and rioting. It had not been that long ago that, while visiting Berl, we had encountered a roadblock of rioting men as we drove into downtown Muskegon. I was concerned as we approached the roadblock and asked my brother, "What are we going to do now?" He turned to me and said, "Hang on to your seat, brother." He pushed the gas pedal of his old Buick to the floor and headed toward the roadblock, honking his horn. I was surprised and relieved that all the men jumped out of the way as we sped by. I wished they would send those troublemakers to Vietnam where they could use that energy to fight the war.

Another letter shared that my brother-in-law Kenneth was at the rifle range at the Marine Corps basic training in San Diego. My in-laws were planning a trip to California to visit both their Marine Corps sons, Tom at Camp Pendleton and Kenneth, who would soon graduate from MCRD in San Diego. My pregnant wife was staying busy with out-of-town relatives from both sides of her family. The Eidson family was having a reunion at Beaver Lake with fishing, boating, skiing, and camping. All those fun activities made me homesick for family and for the beautiful hills of Arkansas.

It was a strange feeling to be at the old French fort, working and standing watch alongside the ARVN. We could not communicate because of the language barrier, but we did manage to converse with our own sign language. We were careful to only fire our weapons when necessary, but the ARVN had a sergeant who had a temper. He went on a screaming rampage, shooting his rifle at some young Vietnamese kids who came daily to search our trash cans. The sergeant ran at them, screaming and firing his rifle in the air. We immediately tried to stop him, explaining that we would all be shot if he continued. He finally understood enough not to shoot again but not before our company commander had screamed at us to "control the idiot!" His angry outburst did not stop the children from scavenging through the trash for food and treasures daily.

Morale was low; we were tired and irritable. It felt like we were on guard duty non-stop because we were short-handed. But the old fort offered one comfort—make-shift showers. These showers were mounted buckets with holes in the bottom that dripped water. We filled the bucket with water, then hurried to soap and rinse before the water ran out. Sometimes we persuaded a buddy to dump extra water into our shower bucket. We stayed dirty because of the constantly blowing wind, filled with dust, grit, and grime. The showers were refreshing and made us feel good to be clean, if only for a little while.

Being on watch was a boring assignment, but we had moments of excitement. One day we captured a Viet Cong informant trying to sneak into the Old Fort as a "friendly." He came unarmed without an ID, so he was escorted into Camp Carroll by one of our squad teams to be interrogated. Early one morning, as my watch was ending, I noticed the village chief coming toward our position. I asked the on-duty guards to watch me as I walked out to meet him. He was upset and agitated as he tried to communicate with me. We called our ARVN friends over to help us interpret what he was trying to say. They told us someone in his village was very sick. Our commander allowed us to send out a squad with a corpsman to see if he could help. The sick person had some type of virus with a fever, so the corpsman gave him some medicine to help the fever and speed up the healing process.

Days had passed without a food drop, and we were getting low on C-rations. A case of C-rations had twelve meals, with an assortment of main courses, such as beefsteak, beans and wieners, chicken and noodles, ham and lima beans, etc. For some reason our food was disappearing at a speedy rate. We wondered if rats could be dragging packages from open boxes and eating them. Then we realized it was the full, unopened boxes of rations that were disappearing. We wondered, *Was it the ARVN?* We were not sure, but the answer came one afternoon when three of the ARVN motioned for me and three other Marines to follow them into their cement bunker. Although they constantly begged us for food and cigarettes, we had finally convinced them that we had neither. They motioned for us to sit down in the bunker, and they left for a few minutes. When they returned, they brought us pineapples and other fruit, cigarettes, and some of our own C-rations. We thanked them and headed back to our post. As we walked away, I realized that they didn't mind taking advantage of us as long as we had plenty of food, but when we had nothing, they were more than willing to share with us, even though it was stolen property.

17

MARILYN'S BIRTHDAY

Marilyn's birthday on July 31st was a sad day for me in more than one way. I missed getting to celebrate with her, and I was also reminded that I would never see her pregnant with our baby. The homesickness was overwhelming, making holidays and birthdays the hardest times to cope with being away from home and my loved ones. I wanted to do something special for Marilyn, so I asked my sister Myra to send her a dozen red roses on her birthday. A few weeks later I received a letter from Marilyn sharing how the roses had been a sweet surprise, making her birthday the best day possible without me.

Marilyn stayed busy preparing for our baby, sewing clothes for herself, baby clothes, and blankets. She and her dad were refinishing furniture for the nursery. We dreamed of our future together as a family as we looked forward to buying a home of our own when I returned. It wasn't realistic, but I continued to hope that somehow, someway I could be home for the delivery of our baby. Our letters to each other were repetitious, "Please be careful, stay safe, don't worry, I love you, miss you, and can't wait to be home." Letters from home boosted my morale, giving me encouragement as I heard from family and friends.

Two ways that I knew the week had ended and Sunday had rolled around again was that a Chaplain would arrive for church services or we were given our malaria prevention meds. The services were interdenominational with only ten to fifteen men usually attending. It was a bit different from back home but it was good to hear the Bible taught and to receive communion. Our church at home had around seven hundred members but the sad part was only about half of them attended each week. I determined then that when I returned home, our family would make God and His church a priority, I wanted us to be faithful to Him and to seek His council for the rest of our lives. I felt close to God during these services with a deep appreciation for His presence with me and His gift of salvation. After seeing so many men die, I couldn't help but wonder if they had known the Lord and had trusted Him for their salvation. I hoped they had made the decision to trust Christ long before the battlefield, because I wanted them to spend eternity in heaven after all they had been through in Vietnam.

> **And we know that in all things God works for the good of those who love Him, who have been called according to his purpose.**
> **(Romans 8:28 NIV)**

18

BACK TO CAMP CARROLL

August 7, 1967. We had been at D-5 camp almost three weeks when we received orders to return to Camp Carroll. This was good news, but before we could return, we were to make a search and destroy sweep from D-5 back to Camp Carroll. We loaded up with our gear and began our sweep. The heat was unbearable as we walked uphill and downhill with heavy loads. I was the gunner and squad leader, so I carried the base plate, barrel, several mortar rounds, my rifle and personal gear like a pack mule. Camp Carroll was our division headquarters where we stored our sea bags. I was anxious to get back so I could get into my sea bag to find my reel to reel tape player and recorder. Marilyn and I made voice recordings to send back and forth in the mail. I was looking forward to hearing her sweet southern voice.

Back at Camp Carroll we were told we would be in the camp for one to two months. While we were there, we were expected to keep clean, take showers, shave and wear clean clothes. That sounded great to me since I was tired of being grubby and wearing my clothes until they literally wore out. Having an occasional shower and eating "almost hot" food was a treat. The mortar attack and sniper fire continued as we stood perimeter watch, but we had the pleasure of sleeping on a cot inside a tent with a bomb shelter nearby. This was much better than sleeping on the ground. Thirteen days later it was depressing to hear we would be leaving Camp Carroll to be a part of Operation Kingfisher.

Blood, Sweat and Honor

August 17, 1967. Operation Kingfisher involved three companies: my Company, Bravo, along with Charlie and Alpha of the 1st Battalion, 9th Marines, 3rd Marine Division. Operation Kingfisher would be a search and destroy mission using four tanks and a scout dog. The sweep would take three weeks. Bravo Company was still short of men, but we felt more confident with the additional help. As the sweep began we found lots of propaganda pamphlets dropped by American planes, as well as pamphlets from the NVA. Both sides used the pamphlets for harassment. Some were left by Bravo and other companies as we passed through the area. Each day our sweep started around 0600 hours and continued until dark. At that point we would dig our foxholes and eat our C-rations. All day long we tromped through the jungle on the lookout for the VC and NVA. At night as we tried to sleep, we could hear them searching for us. It was a "hide-and-seek" type of war where we had to always be ready in case we were found. It felt like we spent days and weeks just looking for trouble. Sadly some of the men were killed or wounded by snipers, some caught in ambushes, and others stepped on mines or fell into a punji pit.[10] During the sweep we discovered an enemy base camp that included thirty bunkers and fighting holes with mortar positions. We destroyed the camp and captured a variety of enemy weapons, including AK-47 rifles, machine guns, and several bundles of medical supplies. We captured one NVA posing as a civilian while carrying Chinese maps and personnel papers. He was immediately sent to the rear for interrogation.

The sun relentlessly bore down on us with the 115 degree temperature causing sunburned faces and arms. The mosquitoes and other insects were a nuisance, causing some of the men to have a mass of sores from the bites. The mosquitoes liked me; I just couldn't keep away from them. They were constantly biting me. At night the temperature would drop into the high 70s with wind and rain making the night miserable. It was hard to sleep. Wearing our ragged clothes, we were a tattered-looking group of men, suffering from lack of food and not enough water. We were constantly moving in the jungle.

---

[10] "A very sharp bamboo stake that is concealed at an angle in high grass, in a hole, or in deep mud, often coated with excrement, and planted to wound and infect the feet of enemy soldiers." The free dictionary by Farlex

Our water came from awful-looking, mosquito-infested mud holes and rice paddies. We were thankful we had Halazone tablets to kill the germs.[11] Even though it left a terrible chlorine taste in your mouth, when you are hot and thirsty you will drink about anything. It wasn't long before we came upon a vacant village that had a well. Two Marines ran over and dropped the bucket in and pulled up what they thought was fresh water. As they began to drink, one of the platoon section leaders ran over and knocked it out of their hands, telling them it was poisoned. We had to be careful of anything that seemed convenient because it could be a booby trap or an ambush.

I felt tired, dull, and years older than I was. My energy and emotions seemed to be dripping from me with each drop of sweat. The constant heat and the stress of the war took its toll on me, but God was my strength. I could trust Him to keep me going, knowing He would never leave me.

> ***God has said, "Never will I leave you;***
> ***never will I forsake you.***
> ***(Hebrews 13:5b)***

As we pressed on, we discovered a little patch of pineapples. We dug them up and peeled them with our K-bar knives. The pineapples tasted so sweet, and, we gorged ourselves, not realizing that we were covering our lips and faces with the juice and acid that caused pain for the next several days. But the taste was worth it. Later in the afternoon, we stopped for our C-ration lunch break.

I found a large, tall mound of dirt to lean back against, making a perfect place to rest and enjoy my lunch. Before long I was told that I was leaning against a Vietnamese grave as some of the Vietnamese people buried their dead in a standing position. I didn't want to be disrespectful, but I was too tired to move.

Marine replacements continued to be added to Bravo Company, bringing us back to full capacity. PFC John Gunning was one of the men assigned to our 60mm mortar section. He was a tall, confident Marine from Winnetka, Illinois. Like many others joining our company, John had not seen combat yet. Right away John and I developed a lifetime friendship. He was funny, easy to talk to, and a

---

[11] A white, crystalline powder, with a strong taste and smell of chlorine, usually used in tablet form to disinfect small quantities of drinking water.

great Marine. We spent many fox-hole and bunker hours talking about home and our families.[12]

Another new Marine looked like a hardware salesman when he arrived. He brought with him a tent, blankets, canned goods, pogie bait (candy), and pots and pans. His plan was to be comfortable. After he carried the extra supplies for a couple of days in the intense heat, hiking up and down the hills, through the rivers and rice paddies, he realized he had too much to carry. He began sharing his canned fruit, candy, and other goodies with the guys. He buried the heaviest items in his foxhole. After a few days he looked like the rest of us, only carrying the necessities of war. We carried only what we needed to survive.

---

[12] Over forty years later we would reconnect through the Internet and meet again in New York City for lunch to reminisce. We still keep in touch by phone and e-mail.

19

REST AND RELAXTION

Finally I had official orders for In-Country R&R (Rest and Relaxation). My orders stated that I was authorized to proceed to China Beach Recreation Center in Da Nang for a period of three days. The orders stated there would be no expense to the government for my travel or food. I was to have sufficient funds in my possession to defray the expenses while I enjoyed my R&R. A minimum of $15.00 was suggested for this trip. I was to leave my personal weapon on padlock and take with me enough clothes for three days. I wasn't sure where I was supposed to get the extra clothes, but that little problem was not keeping me from this trip. I was thrilled to be going and quickly gathered up my gear. I hitched a ride on a helicopter, and as we lifted off, I was reminded again of the devastation this small country had endured. From the air I could see the bomb craters for miles as we flew toward Da Nang. There I caught a bus and headed for China Beach. As we rode along we passed a group of cement buildings similar to apartment complexes back home with screen doors and portable air conditioners in the windows. I was amazed to see that this was where the airmen lived. We passed some airmen walking by, wearing their polished boots, starched utilities, wristwatches, and sunglasses and puffing on American cigarettes. All I could think about was our company of men with their worn-out boots, utilities, old flak jackets, and the used-up gear we were using to fight this war. At first I was angry, but then I felt a sense of pride, knowing that as combat Marines, we were fighting a war and winning most of the battles using worn-out equipment.

China Beach was wonderful! I stayed in a building with divided rooms and window screens. I only had the clothes on my back, but I slept on a cot with a mattress and took real showers. Still it was hard to sleep at night, listening for gunfire and explosions and constantly fearing death. I did not have to get up for a watch or stay on alert during the night. I was pretty much on my own to come and go as I pleased. The mess hall furnished us with three square meals a day, and we could have all we wanted to eat. My favorite treats were the burgers and shakes sold at a small hut off the base. It was hard to realize I was in a place of safety where there were no incoming mortar and rocket attacks and I did not have to fear being shot or hit with shrapnel. It was too good to be true.

On Sunday afternoon we enjoyed a USO show with civilians from the US.[13] It was fun to hear them sing, laugh, and tell jokes. The show was entertaining, and I almost forgot I was in the middle of a war. I had heard about USO shows entertaining the troops, but they were never in our area. They only performed at large bases like Da Nang and Cam Ranh Bay. That was my first and last USO show, and I enjoyed it.

The beach was gorgeous and relaxing. Swimsuits were provided so we could swim in the water and lie on the beach. It felt odd to be on a beach without any women. This was a "men only" beach. It didn't matter to me; it was good to be out of the field, able to relax on a beach. It was a refreshing three days, and I felt rested and relaxed. I was not ready to go back to the bush, but my time was up. Again the chopper picked me up and dropped me off in the field with my company.

The guys were eager to tell me about the battle that I had missed. For many of them, it was their first. They had been attacked by the VC, but none of our men had been injured, and they had sent the VC running. They informed me how LCorp Richard Knee stood in the open on a hill inside the perimeter where he could see the

---

[13] The United Service Organizations Inc. (USO Show) is a nonprofit organization that provides programs, services and live entertainment to United States troops and their families. From Wikipedia, the free encyclopedia

location of the VC and directed the mortar fire. It was a miracle that he was not shot. He was a big guy on his second tour of Vietnam. On his first tour, he was a dog handler in Da Nang. He didn't see much danger, so he volunteered for his second tour. He had a rude awakening when he ended up in our 60mm mortar section with Bravo Company, 1st Battalion, 9th Marine Regiment, traveling with the grunts into the bush. He had heard of Bravo 1/9's reputation of always being in the thick of battle. He had not expected to end up with us, but he adapted just as the rest of us had.

Propaganda Leaflets

20

OPERATION KINGFISHER

August 28, 1967. We traveled back to Camp Carroll where I learned that I had been promoted to Corporal E4 on the first of the month. During formation on August 29, I was presented with my promotion and given a handshake by our captain. Then I was informed that I was officially our mortar squad leader, even though I had already been acting as squad leader for several weeks. The squad leader position was normally held by a corporal or a sergeant, but we did whatever we needed to do to keep the "Big Green Machine" (the Marine Corps) working. I was glad to get the promotion because it would mean more money to send home to Marilyn. We were also introduced to a new section leader who had transferred in. Sgt Robert Brown, from Pennsylvania, he was a twenty-two year old, tall and healthy-looking Marine. A "good ol' boy," he was well-liked by all his men, but he didn't keep his rifle clean, which could create a problem down the road. As I've mentioned before, the M-16 is a good rifle, but it had to stay clean to function properly. Normally the section leader position would have been filled with a lieutenant, but being short-handed, Sergeant Brown filled the position. We were all relieved to see our mortar section being built back up.

After a few days on watch duty at Camp Carroll, our company was assigned to a new location about six miles outside a rural village called Cam Low. Our mission was to keep the VC and NVA miles away from the village to allow the Vietnamese to have their elections on September 3rd. We arrived, set up our perimeter, and dug our foxholes. We thought we were ready for the evening, but orders came for us to move to the other side of Cam Low and dig in again for better security. By the time we finished settling in, it was getting late, and I began making myself some C-ration coffee. I had developed a liking for the awful stuff, and I carried a makeshift cup in my pack. I used a C-ration can as the cup and bent the lid to make the handle. I always had plenty of coffee because many of the guys didn't like the coffee and saved their packs for me. Just as I began to have my first sip we were bombarded by mortar rounds dropping into our perimeter, throwing shrapnel everywhere. We quickly returned mortar fire, but the VC were already gone. This is what they did best—hit and run. They were good at this game. We had no recordable injuries this time. My coffee cup was full of dirt, and it was starting to rain. It looked to be another miserable night under the poncho. We were on 75 percent alert because of the attack; that meant not much sleep. By the time I dropped off to sleep, someone would be kicking my boots, telling me to get up for my watch.

Monsoon season was in full swing, giving us many wet, miserable days and nights. Monsoon began in April and lasted off and on until October. Some days were cloudy with light rain; other days were just a steady downpour. The maximum rainfall was between September and January. The weather in Vietnam was rather sultry and oppressive with high humidity. I should have taken the advice of my good friend Pete Peterson. I had served with him at Camp Lejeune; he had already done his time in Vietnam. His advice was, when it started to rain in Vietnam, to just lay out all my gear, let it get soaked, and not to worry about trying to keep anything dry. Actually that's the way it happened without my trying because we were out in the weather most of the time. It seemed strange to be so hot during the day and then to be so cold at night. After dark we felt like we were freezing because of the drop in temperature and our wet clothes.

We felt better prepared having our four tanks and an 81mm mortar section with us. Food was scarce, so we were eager to see the helicopters flying in for a food drop. At the same time, we dreaded what we knew was coming. The helicopters identified our position to the enemy, so we knew the mortar and rocket attacks would soon begin. As the helicopters arrived they barely had time to kick out the cases of C-rations and cans of water and then to lift off. Marines were designated to run out to get our supplies as we heard the usual *thump, thump, thump* of mortars being fired. The men were barely able to retrieve the supplies and get back into their fox holes before the mortar rounds exploded all around us. For about ten minutes we hugged the ground inside our foxholes, praying that we would not get a direct hit. Thank God, He answered our prayers. We worked hard at locating the enemy position and then we began dropping our 60mm mortar rounds back on them. In a few minutes the enemy would be gone, carrying with them their dead and wounded. We then searched their positions, finding blood stains on the ground and drag marks from the bodies, as well as the mortar craters from our rounds.

We returned to Camp Carroll to await further assignment. I was looking forward to the opportunity to send home some film, write letters, and make a recorded audio reel for Marilyn. After sorting through my mail, I found a reel and a letter from her, along with other letters from my in-laws, my mom, and another recording from our friends Sharon and Dee Spann. As I read Marilyn's letter and heard her voice, it was like someone giving me a hot fudge sundae but not allowing me to eat it. Hearing her voice and reading the letters made me homesick. I listened to the recording of her voice saying, "I love you." Wow, that was good! I played the tape over and over again. Hearing her voice made me want to go AWOL by catching the next plane headed home. I could sympathize with Marines who made that choice after being away from home for so long.

It was good to be stationed back at Camp Carroll even though our missions took us outside the perimeter for two to three days at a time. We made daily sweeps along with search and destroy missions, but then we would return to camp at night to a tent and cots. It rained constantly the last three days we were out from camp. We soon became tired of tromping through water and mud. Digging a foxhole was hard because the water quickly filled it up. We were miserable sitting in knee-deep muddy water, while taking incoming rounds.

The next stop was called The Rock. This place had several bunkers already built in the area. A river was close by, so we enjoyed taking a swim, having a bath, and having a place to wash our clothes. We had orders to spend three weeks at The Rock, but those orders changed while we ate our noon C-rations. Back to Camp Carroll we went. I had mail waiting and pictures of Marilyn with her little round belly. She was only two and a half months from delivering our baby, and she looked great. I picked out a picture to carry with me and sent the rest back home because I knew they would be damaged by all the dampness.

My brother-in-law Tommy was home on leave from Camp Pendleton. He wanted to come to Vietnam in place of his younger brother, Kenneth. Kenneth was at ITR and still anxious to get to the war and shoot some VC. I did not want to discourage him, but war is nothing like what you expect. It is no picnic. Tommy was willing to serve and did receive orders for Vietnam on two different occasions. The first time they were changed for unknown reasons, but the second time the orders were denied because his brother was already in Vietnam.

September 15th through the 18th we were on a search and destroy operation in the Cam Lo Valley north of the Cam Lo River, using Hill 100 and the ridge line as our guides for cover. We occupied a position at the Khe Gia Bridge. Our biggest enemy around the bridge came from the heavy rains that caused the rivers and streams to flood. Bunkers and positions were flooded, making it a real quagmire. We busied ourselves by digging drainage ditches and reinforcing the defensive wire around our position. We were unprepared for this season of monsoon rain storms. During one downpour we were using our ponchos to construct a makeshift tent when a tear gas grenade went off close by. We had a quick lesson in putting on our gas masks, an item we always carried but rarely used. We had to dump the dirt from our masks and then put them on as fast as we could. We later learned one of our own men had accidentally set off the grenade.

Back at Camp Carroll on September 24th, we received a rocket attack with forty-three rounds of 102mm rockets that destroyed our position, killing two of our Marines and wounding ten. We returned mortar fire, stopping the attack but leaving no recordable results.

The first day of October found us waiting on a supply truck for a delivery of food and ammunition to our unit. The truck driver ran over a 7.5 mine that blew the vehicle into the air, totaling it. Fortunately, the driver survived with minor injuries. On our next sweep out and around the camp, we found ten bunkers that looked to be about two-weeks old with construction tools inside. We destroyed the bunkers with C-4.

During mail call I received all the stuff I had asked Marilyn to send me: plastic bags to keep personal items dry, Kool-Aid to make the water bearable to drink, and a green rain suit to help keep me dry during this unending rain. We all had a good laugh when my friend, John Gunning, opened his mail to find two white ponchos with little brown ducks sprinkled all over. His poor mom did not realize the white ponchos made him a walking target for the gooks. He kiddingly sent the ponchos back to his mom with a question, "Mom, did you really need my insurance that bad?" Later she sent him the dark green ponchos similar to mine. Poor John was harassed about the duck ponchos for a long time by his fellow Marines, including our section leader, Sergeant Brown.

Our next assignment was to move our division headquarters from Camp Carroll back to Dong Ha. Our fighting unit would be going to Con Thien again to spend some "Time in the Barrel" and to protect the "Hill of Angels." The preparation, packing up, and moving our headquarters took three days.

The morning of October 4th, we were told that General Westmoreland had announced to the folks back home we had gained a victory at Con Thien, stating that the NVA had moved back, leaving their gun sites and positions. I was thinking, *Wake up, General. Those gooks move around all the time to attempt to fool us. They aren't gone; they will be back.*

After re-reading some letters from Marilyn I was reminded that in a little over a month, I would be a dad. Our baby was due to be born in November, and the time was getting close. In four months I would be going home, and by then we would be a family of three. The thought of home was so very exciting; it was hard to wait. I still yearned to be home for the birth of our baby, but I didn't want to feel sorry for myself. I knew I was not the first Marine or soldier to be at war when his child was born. I was very thankful and fortunate that Marilyn had both our parents to support her during the pregnancy and the birth of our baby. It was fun to think about names, and we finally settled on two: For a girl, Cynthia Carolyn. Both were family names. Cynthia was Marilyn's great-grandmother and Carolyn was after her older sister Nancy Carolyn Gettig, who had been killed in a car wreck. If the baby was a boy, we would name him Christopher Derl after me. Our main concern and prayer, of course, was for a healthy baby.

During October 5th and 6th, we received a hail storm of incoming rounds, sixty-six rounds of mixed artillery and mortar fire that managed to tear up our hillside and wound eleven Marines. There never seemed to be a safe place where the enemy would not strike. We just hoped and prayed that the next bomb would not land on our bunker

Richard Knee, Simon Cull, Derl Horn at Con Thien

21
BACK TO CON THIEN

October 10, 1967. A few days after moving our 1/9 command post to Dong Ha, we began our travel back to Con Thien. The rain was relentless, and the mud collected on our boots, making it difficult to walk. With each step we sank up to our ankles in mud. It helped to have my rain suit. It gave me some protection from the monsoon rain. The downside was that the suit was hot, making me as wet with sweat as I would have been with the rain. I could not win with the miserable weather in Vietnam.

We were on a four-day search and destroy mission from Dong Ha to Con Thien. Each night we sent out our rifle team patrols, then moved our company during the day. We were on the move, daily digging new positions. It was not an easy assignment to dig a mud hole large enough for our mortar and two men. By the time we finished digging our fox holes and setting up our mortar for patrol support, we would find our foxholes half-full of water again. As we moved closer to Con Thien, the mud got deeper. If my boots were not tied securely they would be left in the mud. It was a battle just to walk and not fall down with all the weight we were packing. As we moved into the Con Thien perimeter, we passed another company leaving. It was 2nd Battalion, 3rd Marines, and I recognized Morris Sears, a Marine I served with back at Camp Lejeune. It was good to see a familiar face, but we did not have much time to talk, other than to trade mailing addresses.

The mortar position we were assigned to maintain looked rundown, but at least we had a bunker. Our assignment for the next few weeks was to help protect Con Thien and to give 60mm mortar support to our Marines as they went on patrols. The ground was wet and muddy. We knew we would be taking incoming mortar and rockets soon, so we immediately began working on the bunker and digging a mortar pit. For days we worked on reinforcing it with sandbags and dirt-filled wooden mortar boxes. We had no sooner set up our mortars and unpacked our gear when we heard the *thump, thump, thump* of mortars firing in the distance. We all crammed inside the bunker and held our breath and our ears as we prayed we would not take a direct hit. We knew it was not strong enough for a direct hit. As soon as there was a lull in the mortar attack, we ran out and returned mortar fire into the enemy location, hoping for a secondary explosion. When we saw the big explosion with lots of black smoke billowing into the sky, we knew that we had made a direct hit on their ammo dump, destroying their position and most likely killing most of the enemy. It made us feel a bit safer for a short time.

During the next two days, we worked every chance we had to improve our bunker. The records indicated that we took in 105 rounds of mixed artillery, mortar, and recoilless rifle rounds, killing two of our Marines and wounding seventeen. Again we had a lot of shrapnel and bullet holes that damaged the bunker so our squads took turns repairing and improving it as we continued firing mortar rounds back at the VC in the wooded areas surrounding Con Thien.

At night we attempted to rest between our two-man watches that lasted for three hours. One night Sergeant Brown and I had the watch from 2300 hours until 0200 hours. Some evenings the VC would leave us alone at night, making for a quiet and boring evening. On one such night, I was leaning back against the bunker about half asleep when a dirty little mouse dropped from the top of the bunker onto my head, down my nose and face, giving me an adrenalin rush and earning a big laugh from Sergeant Brown. Seeing that little mouse reminded me of how fearful Marilyn was of those little furry creatures.

At nine months pregnant, she saw a mouse in the house and jumped up on the kitchen counter. Since her parents were at work, she called my mom to come to her rescue. Mom arrived but the little critter had disappeared. Her dad did not believe it was a mouse since they had never had one in the home. That night as he relaxed in his recliner, the brave little mouse made his appearance from down the hall. All the family saw him and the chase was on. Soon that was the end of the little mouse. Right after we were married, I caught three mice in our apartment. Thinking I could help "cure" Marilyn of her fear, I attempted to show her how harmless they were, but that only made matters worse. From that point on, I just took care of the mice.

On October 12, 1967 a group of newsmen came to Con Thien to interview some Marines involved in the July 2 battle, Operation Buffalo. They told us the report might be on the news but it was mainly for Marine Corps records. They never made it to our position, so I did not give them my two cents worth. An article and picture appeared later in *Newsweek* magazine, July 17, 1968, about the ambush along the DMZ where we lost 90 percent of our company.

We continued working hard on our bunker; it was state of the art when we finished. We made good use of our empty mortar ammo boxes, tearing them apart and using the nails to install a floor and walls in our bunker. We not only had a bunker but we had floors and walls. We were then sleeping on wood instead of dirt. The wood was hard but a lot cleaner than the wet dirt.

We each had our own sleeping spots. Sometimes we even took off our boots, but only when we all participated because of the odor. Feet that stay inside boots for weeks at a time can produce an unbearable stench. Without our boots, the mice and rats found our toes inviting to chew on during the night.

The weather was almost unbearable. Though not as awful as the summer months, we had come to expect the heat and humidity. We were having a moderate monsoon week with rain mostly during the night, only stopping in the early morning hours and leaving us with plenty of mud. Rebuilding our bunkers in the rain and mud was difficult, but we worked hard. We hoped to make it secure enough to withstand a direct hit from a mortar or rocket, even though we knew there was no guarantee.

Mortars and rockets continued to fall on our position, and we crowded our sweaty bodies inside the bunker. The humid air was thick, making it hard to breath. It was difficult to locate the enemy positions due to the rain and the camouflaged brush they hid behind

22

KILLING OUR OWN

During the morning hours on Friday, October 13th at Con Thien, we received 105 mortar, rocket, and 57mm recoilless rifle rounds within our perimeter, causing major damage to our bunkers and gun positions. We were also harassed by sporadic sniper fire.

In the early afternoon friendly bombs[14] were accidentally dropped on the inside of our battalion perimeter by an A-4 Sky hawk.[15] This caused bunkers to cave in, burying Marines and injuring others with shrapnel. Our bunker survived without a cave-in, but we bounced around like rubber balls for a few minutes. Two men were killed, PO George Everett Shade of H&S company and Pfc Herman Benard Gailliard of Delta company; seventeen men were wounded before the strikes could be called off.

---

[14] Friendly fire is an attack by a military force on friendly forces while attempting to attack the enemy, either misidentifying the target as hostile, or due to errors or inaccuracy. Such attacks often cause injury or death. From Wikipedia, the free encyclopedia.

[15] The Skyhawk is a light-weight aircraft with a maximum takeoff weight of 24,500 pounds (11,100 kg) and has a top speed of more than 600 miles per hour (970 km/h). The aircraft's five hard points support a variety of missiles, bombs and other munitions and was capable of delivering nuclear weapons using a low altitude bombing system and a "loft" delivery technique. The A-4 was originally powered by the Wright J65 turbojet engine; from the A-4E onwards, the Pratt & Whitney J52 was used.

Sergeant (E5) Phil Sutherland, Section leader with the 106mm recoilless rifle platoon in H&S (Headquarters and Service) company at Con Thien

"On October 13 our 106mm recoilless rifle platoon is here in support of the rifle platoons and guarding the perimeter at Con Thien. Our recoilless rifle is very effective against ground troops in the open with its flechette rounds carrying 9,000 darts that could be set to explode at a desired distance up to 2,000 yards.[16] We did not know at the time, but there was a buildup going on in the area to the north of the DMZ and into the Trace just north of Con Thien in preparation of the Tet attack in January 1968. The NVA were probing and testing our strength and trying to soften us up for Tet. It was not uncommon for us to have as many as 800 rounds coming in a day. We were calling in air strikes for the B-52 planes which usually do a tremendous job with their bombs but did not seem to have an effect on the enemy positions this time. The A-4 Skyhawk fighter planes were called in to bomb the area where the artillery was coming from. I was sitting outside on the edge of my bunker watching from my gun position for NVA troops when the A-4 came screaming down, firing its nose cannon into the barbed wire surrounding Con Thien on the west side about 25 meters out and then on the east side. The plane circled around and dropped several bombs by mistake inside the compound at Con Thien, killing some Marines and wounding others. I was one of the wounded. One of the bombs landed about 25 yards behind me between the two hills where most of the shrapnel was absorbed. The bomb exploded upward in a V angle, and some shrapnel shredded the back of my flak jacket and helmet. I was blown up into the air and landed on the ground unconscious. I ended up with a leg and head wound. My wounds were treated and I was medevaced out by helicopter to Phu Bai where they further treated me and put a cast on my leg from my hips to my toes and bandaged my head. After several days the cast was removed and I was released to go back to my battalion rear area in

---

[16] A flechette is a pointed steel projectilewith a vaned tail for stable flight. From Wikipedia, the free encyclopedia

Dong Ha just in time for the Marine Corps Birthday feast. I love shrimp so I had a double serving of spoiled shrimp which made me deathly sick. They shipped me back to Phu Bai where I was in the hospital for several more weeks and then released to go home to the States."

■■

The next day was even more difficult as the enemy hurled 190 more rounds from mortars and rockets into our positions, causing more death and destruction. Our days were spent inside our bunkers, and we only came out to fire our mortars back into the enemy positions. After a time of firing our mortars and using all the other big guns, we managed to quiet the enemy for a few hours. During the lull we were busy caring for our wounded and dead, and then we turned our attention to repairing the damage done to our positions.

On October 15th we began platoon and company sweeps 1,000 meters out from Con Thien to the East, South, Southwest, and Western areas to keep the enemy mortar and small arms fire to a minimum. This allowed our engineers time to set up minefields to try to keep the enemy from the battalion's outer wire. It was obvious to all of us that the NVA were building up their forces around Con Thien. Our commander called in air strikes that promptly set off eleven secondary explosions, helping to slow down the incoming rounds for a few days.

Our battalion did a four-day sweep from October 26th to the 29th where we discovered numerous bunkers, rifles, ammunition, explosives, gas masks and propaganda sheets outside our perimeter. We destroyed them all. October was a sad and discouraging month at Con Thien as we had twelve men killed and 155 wounded from all the bombing.

Marilyn wrote that our unborn baby was very active and would arrive in about five weeks. It was hard to imagine that I would be a dad, but I felt sure it was a role I would enjoy. I was anxious to meet that little person. She also shared that they were having a beautiful fall season with the leaves changing and nice, cool weather. I missed life in the Ozarks. With the fall season came football games, and our favorite team was the Arkansas Razorbacks. On Saturday they had just won their game against Texas Christian University 26 to 0.

Woooooooooooo Pig Sooie!

I also learned that my brother-in-law Kenneth was home on leave and would be going to staging in preparation for deployment to Vietnam. He was to arrive in-country sometime in November. I hated to see him come to Vietnam because he was so young, as were most Marines, and I didn't want to see him go through the anguish I had experienced for the last several months. Kenneth wrote asking for advice upon his arrival in Vietnam. I told him to pay close attention to the advice of his leaders and the salty, experienced Marines; to stay alert at all times; to keep his rifle clean; to dig deep holes; and most of all, to pray a lot. Only God could bring him through the experience.

Other news from home was disappointing. My mom was filing for a divorce from my dad. I didn't blame her. I knew it was the result of my dad going through a mid-life crisis, but it was difficult and sad to think my parents would never be together again and my family would never be the same. As children we had enjoyed a happy home, and we knew we were loved. I found it tough to deal with these issues, being ten thousand miles away from home.

I was thankful to know there were many good folks back home praying for me and for my protection, as well as for the other Marines and servicemen who were fighting. The frustrating news was how people were protesting the war back home. This made me sick to my stomach, realizing that so many of our countrymen were not supporting us while we were risking our lives for their protection, their freedom, and to prevent the growth of Communism.

The North Vietnamese commanders must have been happy to read U.S. newspaper reports of the rioting and unrest among the anti-war protesters. They were rallying on almost every college campus in the United States. General Giap and Ho Chi Minh were counting on the cowards in our universities and the news media to infect the people with hopelessness and panic. It was reported that General Giap recognized that the American servicemen had shown implacable bravery over and over again against their best troops, with the U.S. winning most of the battles. It was also said that he wondered how a country could produce such brave, fearless warriors who were heroic in their fight, but then produce so many spoiled brats and crybabies on our colleges and university campuses. His hope in a victory for Communism was for the U.S. to grow tired of the war and to pull out of Vietnam. Those under his leadership worked hard at maintaining the lie that Vietnam was united and the conflict was only a civil war and not a Communist takeover and expansion. I felt if we were willing to travel ten thousand miles to help the South Vietnamese, we should be ready to go the distance and willing to do whatever it took to win the war. After seeing the destruction and suffering of war, I was willing to fight anywhere outside our home country.

It was heartbreaking to witness families losing their loved ones, their homes, their businesses, their dignity, and their hope as they suffered terrible abuse at the hands of the enemy. The protesters back home didn't understand the brutality and deception of the Viet Cong and the North Vietnamese to their southern cousins. If the American public could only see the truth about what was happening to these families, I felt they would support us in our fight to free South Vietnam from Communism and to stop it from spreading into the U.S. and other countries.

At mail call I received an "in-country" letter from my Marine buddy Ronald Kist who was with 60mm mortars in 2nd Battalion, 4th Marine Regiment. Ron and I had served together in the states and in Okinawa. He updated me with news of our mutual Marine buddies. One friend, Walker, had given Ron my address, and he shared that Helmic and Loupias were in Echo Company of 2/4, Juby was in Hotel Company, and Robinson was in 2/3. Helmic had been injured in the face with shrapnel but was doing okay. Juby had been hit in both arms with shrapnel but was all right. He had heard that I had a baby boy, but of course Marilyn was only pregnant. His battalion had been hit hard as they maneuvered outside of Con Thien. It was good to get news that my friends were making it through this war. I missed my buddies. They were the ones I had trained with before coming to Vietnam, but after we arrived we were separated.

We continued to have plenty of activity by the NVA around Con Thien as they dropped mortars and rockets on us. Air strikes were called in, and the F-4 jets would roar in as they dropped their 500-pound bombs on the NVA. When they scored a hit on the enemy position or ammo storage, they would signal us as they flew by with a victory roll.[17] What a beautiful sight! After dark we continued to receive small arms fire and mortars. Our AC-47 aircraft that Marines called "Puff, the Magic Dragon" flew over us with its guns blazing.[18] "Puff" could put a 7.62mm slug in every square foot of a football field with a 3-second burst from its three electrically operated miniguns. It was awesome to watch the three solid streams of orange that appeared to be fire, because every fifth round was a tracer round. This plane could fire six thousand rounds per minute, making it look as if it covered the whole area. It was comforting to have "Puff" on our side, and after its arrival, the rest of the evening was quiet. There was no doubt that the NVA were dead or in a deep hole somewhere after that demonstration of firepower. We had been pinned down for twenty-three continuous days without a shave or bath due to the incoming mortar and rocket fire. We were a bunch of dirty, stinking Marines.

October 30. Our mortar section leader, Sergeant Brown, was leaving the field to go home. I was happy for him but hated to see him go. We had become good friends. I would be stepping up to fill his position as a section leader until we had a new sergeant or lieutenant assigned to us. We seemed to be continually short on officers and sergeants, so we were not hopeful about a replacement coming soon.

November 1. We made it through Halloween, and it was just

---

[17] Victory Roll. The aileron roll is an aerobatic maneuver in which the aircraft does a full 360° revolution about its longitudinal axis. When executed properly, there is no appreciable change in altitude and the aircraft exits the maneuver on the same heading as it entered. This is commonly one of the first maneuvers taught in basic aerobatics courses. This maneuver is often incorrectly referred to as a barrel roll. From Wikipedia, the free encyclopedia,

[18] The Douglas AC-47 Spooky (also nicknamed "Puff, the Magic Dragon") was the first in a series of gunships developed by the United States Air Force during the Vietnam War. From Wikipedia, the free encyclopedia.

another day on the Hill of Angels,[19] Con Thien. November is a special month for me because it was the month I met and married Marilyn. At this point, we were expecting our first child and I wondered would our color be blue or pink? Would it be Chris or Cindy? I thought that having a son first would be ideal, so the siblings who followed would have a big brother to look up to like I had enjoyed in my family. Either way this baby would be a blessing from God, and I would be thankful. It was not safe for a married man with a pregnant wife to be serving in Vietnam, as it was difficult not to daydream about my wife, the baby, and home. Daydreaming was a dangerous distraction, keeping me from being alert and watching out for Charlie.[20]

Only twenty-one more days left before the birth of our first child and only 115 days left before leaving Vietnam and the Corps. I was considered a short-timer and it felt good, but it was still a lot of days left to stay alive. The daily average of men killed in action during 1967 was forty-four.

The weather continued to be hot and humid, but we had grown accustomed to it. We were in the middle of a light monsoon season with rain most of the night, then letting up in the early morning hours, generating plenty of mud. We continued to work hard to rebuild our bunkers to withstand a direct hit from a mortar or rocket, but we knew there was never a guarantee that the bunker or any of us would survive.

The VC was actively firing mortars and rockets onto our base, and it was hard to determine their location. We called in the Bird

---

[19]Con Thien (Vietnamese: căn cứ Conn Tiên, meaning the "Hill of Angels"), was a United States Marine Corps combat base located near the Vietnamese Demilitarized Zone about 3 km from North Vietnam. It was the site of fierce fighting from February 1967 through February 1968. Cồn Thien, Gio Linh District, Quảng Trị Province. Wikipedia, the free encyclopedia.
[20] Provisional Revolutionary Government of the Republic of South Vietnam (PRG) People's ... American soldiers referred to the Viet Cong as Victor Charlie or V-C. *Vietnam War Glossary*, by Jennifer Rosenberg. Charlie or Mr. Charlie Slang for Viet Cong (VC). The term is short for the phonetic spelling (used by the military and police to spell things over the radio) of "VC," which is "Victor Charlie."
[20] Provisional Revolutionary Government of the Republic of South Vietnam (PRG) People's ... American soldiers referred to the Viet Cong as Victor Charlie or V-C. *Vietnam War Glossary*, by Jennifer Rosenberg. Charlie or Mr. Charlie Slang for Viet Cong (VC). The term is short for the phonetic spelling (used by the military and police to spell things over the radio) of "VC," which is "Victor Charlie."

Dog observation planes to help us spot their location.[21] The Bird Dog pilots were a special breed of men. They flew around the countryside in a plane that felt about as secure as a tin can. The plane was used to draw enemy fire, allowing us to pinpoint their positions for air strikes or artillery fire. The pilots would spot the enemy and then call in air strikes on the positions marked with white phosphorus bombs. The F-4 Phantom jets would come sweeping in overhead to unload their heavy-duty bombs. The jets would fly back over our position, giving us a victory roll to confirm that they had indeed knocked out the positions. The victory roll always brought a big round of loud cheers of appreciation from those of us on the ground.

November 4. Orders came for Bravo Company to do a sweep around Con Thien the next day. The sweep began before daylight at 0530 hours. We looked for the enemy and anything left to indicate that they had been in the area. All day long we sloshed around in the rain and mud without locating anything other than a bunch of leaflets dropped by the NVA. The leaflets were filled with propaganda attempting to scare us with death threats and discourage us with the suggestion that no one back home supported the war. Although the information was partly true, it did not have the demoralizing effect they had hoped for. On our sweep, we found fruit trees with tangerines, grapefruit, and bananas. Most of the fruit was green except for the delicious tangerines that we enjoyed. We finished the sweep around 1700 hours and ended up back at our positions at Con Thien.

November 6. I was always looking for a way to make our C-rations taste better. I managed to come up with a tasty recipe for a hot meal I called my C-ration hash. The recipe consisted of a can of meatballs with beans, juice from a can of beefsteak, four canned crackers crumbled up, chopped onions (compliments of Sgt. Robert Brown at Dong Ha), and one teaspoon of canned peanut butter. I stirred the ingredients together, heated it, and then enjoyed eating my

---

[21]The Cessna L-19/O-1 Bird Dog was a liaison and observation aircraft. It was the first all-metal fixed-wing aircraft ordered for and by the United States Army since the U.S. Army Air Forces separated from the Army in 1947, becoming its own branch of service, the United States Air Force.. The Bird Dog had a lengthy career in the U.S. military, as well as in other countries. During the Vietnam War 470 of the spotter planes were shot down. From Wikipedia, the free encyclopedia.

meal while washing it down with some good ol' C-ration coffee. Hot food was a treat no matter what it was. With the next food and supply drop, we received an extra supply of water that I used for bathing. It felt refreshing and good to be clean again, especially after giving my feet a good scrubbing. We were also issued clean utilities (shirt and pants), skivvies (undershirt and shorts) and socks, something that didn't happen often enough. Now with our clean clothes and our bath, we were in hog heaven for a few days. I usually wore the socks and skivvies for a week or two, then discarded them and waited for the next supply in three to six weeks.

Along with the new duds, I received a note from my friend, Sgt. Robert Brown, who was waiting at Dong Ha for his flight home. He started his letter with, "Hi Horney" (one of my many nicknames), Enclosed is the twenty dollars that I owe you and thanks." He had gone seven months without receiving his pay, so I had loaned him twenty dollars. When his money finally arrived, he received over twelve hundred dollars. He mentioned that Ronnie Fields was in Dong Ha, recovering from his July 2nd gunshot wounds from our shoot-out with the NVA. He would soon be leaving for R&R, but Brown did not know the location. He also mentioned that John Gunning would be returning to us on November 9th after his R&R. He ended the letter with a promise to write again soon, and he wrote, "Tell everyone hello." He jokingly added, "Tell Tom to get out of the doorway." Tom always sat in the entry of our bunker during down times so he could quickly duck inside the bunker if we had incoming rounds. Brown also reminded us to add more sandbags to the roof of our bunker. According to him we could never have enough sandbags on top of the bunker. He always wanted us to add another layer, as his goal was to keep us safe. The letter made me miss my friend.

November 7. It was a calm, quiet day without much activity, so we spent time cleaning our M-16 rifles and our mortars, and again reinforcing our bunker. We were relaxed and enjoying our day until we heard that old familiar *thump, thump, thump, boom, boom, boom* of mortars and artillery rounds headed our way. We barely had enough time to crowd into our bunker as the rounds pounded around us. Two Marines failed to get into the bunker in time and were wounded by the shrapnel. "Corpsman Up" was a call we heard daily because of the numbers of men who were wounded or killed.[22] The brave chopper pilots faithfully flew in to pick up our dead and wounded. As the choppers arrived, they automatically gave away our location, bringing more attacks of mortars and rockets. When the firing stopped, we hurried out of our bunkers to get our mortars zeroed in by setting the elevation and deflection to return mortar rounds back to the enemy positions. The firing continued back and forth for a couple of hours, but thankfully no one else was killed or injured. We hoped that we had inflicted enough damage on the enemy with the mortars to give us a few hours of peace and quiet. It was an awful experience to see our wounded men in terrible pain. We felt sad to see them flying away from our unit, knowing many would not return. I had a deep appreciation for the medevac helicopter crews who bravely picked up our dead and wounded, even though their arrival meant that soon we would have another bombardment of mortars and rockets. It was frightening to live with the constant fear that the next mortar or rocket might be the one to kill or injure one of us. We recognized that we were only one heartbeat away from death on a daily basis. After the firefights settled, we would usually fall back into a more passive state of mind and feel some relief from the constant fear of facing death so close and so often.

It was hard to settle down after this particular attack. I realized my glasses were missing. The search was on, but my glasses could not be found. This wasn't the first time I was without my glasses. During boot camp they were in my footlocker most of the time because it was difficult to wear them through the training exercises. I had worn glasses for five years due to my impaired vision. I was thankful to have good vision in my right eye, but my left eye vision was poor. My glasses would be replaced when I returned to the States.

It was my turn to stand the last watch of the morning of November 8th, from 0330 hours until daylight at 0630 hours. As I finished my watch, I was tired and sleepy, but also happy that my good friends, John Gunning and Ronnie Fields, would be returning soon from R&R. Their return would shorten the length of our

---

[22] A US Navy Corpsman, wearing the same dirty, torn, and smelly green utilities worn by his Marine brothers and 'armed' with his B-1 medical kit, went to the aid of wounded Marines. Usually under enemy fire, these 'angels in green' performed lifesaving miracles with complete disregard for their own safety. Talking Proud Archives --- Military

watches, and they would have plenty of interesting stories to share with us, giving us some much needed entertainment. In addition to their return, we had new Marines joining our mortar section on November 8th, meaning we would be putting the new men through speed training to prepare them for the battles to come.

News from headquarters was discouraging. We were told that two men from our 60mm mortar squad would be transferring to 81mm mortars. The men did not want to leave our squad, and I was working hard to keep us together since we were already short the number of men we actually needed. I was originally trained in 81mm mortars, but I knew I would not be transferred since I was considered a "short-timer" with only three months left in country. Also I was the most senior and experienced person in 60mm mortars at that time.

The next few days between mortar and rocket attacks, we worked hard improving our bunker, mortar pit and ammo storage. It felt good to have a bunker rather than just a fox hole since a bunker offered more protection. We reinforced it with layers of sandbags and then a layer of mortar round boxes filled with dirt. The mortar pit was positioned in front of our bunker. When the rain started, we had to quickly bail it out to keep it from running back into the bunker.

After Simon Cull, John Gunning, Richard Knee, Tom Hines, and Ronnie Fields returned to our squad, we all worked together to keep the water out of the mortar pit. One day as we bailed out the water, a newsman from *Leatherneck* magazine walked up with his camera. He took a few pictures and asked a few questions. Before he could finish taking notes, we heard the sound of mortars and rockets being fired, forcing us all to rush inside the bunker. The newsman told us the article about Con Thien would be coming out in January, 1968. Later, we would see the picture of all of us in *Leatherneck* magazine, working on our mortar pit and bailing water.

23

MARINE CORPS 199TH BIRTHDAY

November 10, 1967. On the199th birthday of the Marine Corps, the Corps treated us special. I'm not sure how it was accomplished, but they served each of us a hot birthday dinner fit for a king. The menu included steak, boiled shrimp, peas, rolls, cake, milk, sodas, beer, and even ice cream, one of my favorite desserts (even melted). The food tasted delicious going down, but unfortunately we did not know that the shrimp was spoiled. Ninety percent of us succumbed to food poisoning. We were sick all night, "barfing up our heels," and unable to do anything. If the enemy had known of our condition, we would have been helpless to defend ourselves. I did not realize at the time that I would be unable to eat shrimp for the rest of my life. After being sick most of the night, I felt better by early morning and was able to stand my watch at 0400 hours.

The next day, the scoop around camp was that we would be leaving Con Thien on November 15 to go to Camp Evans near Phu Bia, but, as with all rumors, we never knew if they were really true until they actually happened.

Mail call continued to be the most exciting part of the day, and I received letters from Marilyn, my dad, my brother-in-law Tommy, and another letter from my old buddy, Ron Kist. But the best part of mail call that day was the pictures I received of my beautiful, pregnant wife. For several days all I wanted to do was sit and look at her pictures, even though I knew I would have to send them back so they would not be destroyed by the wet weather. I did keep one picture to carry with me and did my best to keep it clean and dry.

My mortar section was close to being at full strength when we learned the 81mm mortar section still needed more men, causing our company commander to transfer some of our Marines. Training was in process when I received notification that my assistant gunner would be moving over to 81mm mortars in the next few days. This placed more pressure on me to finish the training process with the new men so our gun crew would be fully prepared for combat. I prayed they would learn quickly.

Two of the men in our section had been in-country for several months, and they were due for a promotion. They had worked hard and deserved the advancement. I talked with our commander about the possibility of promoting them since one was still a private and the other was a private first class. I was a non-commissioned officer, a corporal at the time, in charge of our mortar section, and I wanted to help my men in any way I could. As a corporal, I had a small amount of influence, but I did my best to see that those men received the promotions they deserved. Eventually the promotions were awarded to them.

Monsoon season finally moved in to stay. The rain poured down daily, causing the mud to get deeper. We were able to get out of the rain while we slept in the bunker or during other times when we were not on watch or having to fire the mortars. I was disappointed when I woke up for my watch at 0100 hours because I was in the middle of a wonderful dream about arriving home. I had run to meet Marilyn and we were holding each other, when I was abruptly awakened by someone kicking my boots and telling me it was my turn to stand watch.

On November 15th, I had only 101 days left in the Corps and only eleven more days until I could become a proud daddy. I was much more excited about the latter.

Our company commander announced that our company had been awarded the Presidential Unit Citation.[23] The award would be

---

[23] The Presidential Unit Citation (PUC), originally called the Distinguished Unit Citation, is awarded to units of the United States Armed Forces, and those of allied countries, for extraordinary heroism in action against an armed enemy on or after 7 December 1941 (the date of the attack on Pearl Harbor and the start of American involvement in World War II). The unit must display such gallantry, determination, and *esprit de corps* in accomplishing its mission under extremely difficult and hazardous conditions so as to set it apart from and above other units participating in the same campaign. From Wikipedia, the free encyclopedia

presented at a later date, but it felt good to know we were going to be recognized for a job well done. It did not remove the sadness I felt from the loss of our Marine buddies who paid the ultimate sacrifice during Operation Buffalo. I was thankful that I had survived but wondered why God spared my life when so many good men had died around me. I would mourn these brave men the rest of my life. Our company was featured in the *Sea Tiger* newspaper,[24] but no one back home would hear of this honor or see the newspaper article. I had seen the newspaper but did not get home with one.

November 15th was also the day we were scheduled to move to Camp Evans, but it did not happen. The new date was to be November 17, but I was not counting on that date either. Instead of leaving for Camp Evans on the 17th, we received orders to make a company-wide sweep around Con Thien. We left early in the morning and returned late afternoon. The mission was to make sure that the enemy had no positions outside our perimeter. At the conclusion of the day, we only found a few positions left behind by the enemy. The miserable monsoon rain beat down on us, soaking us and making it difficult to walk in the thick, sticky mud as it created a suction that pulled at our boots. It was frustrating to think that the enemy was probably enjoying their day in a dry tunnel.

November 18th was a special day for me. It marked the anniversary of my first date with Marilyn back in 1960. It was a blind date set up by friends of ours, Truman Brewer and his girlfriend Brenda Brown (Baker). Truman told me to call and ask Marilyn out for a date as he thought she would accept. I had graduated from Springdale High School in 1960, and I was working at the AQ Chicken House restaurant in Springdale. I was shy and nervous about talking with Marilyn, but I decided that as soon as I had a break from work, I would call and invite her out. When I called, her mother answered the phone. I asked to speak to her daughter, and she asked me which one. I drew a blank. I could not remember her name, so I said, "your youngest daughter," knowing she had an older sister, Nancy Carolyn Buchanan. When Marilyn answered the phone, I invited her to go with me to the junior play at the Field House on the Springdale High School campus. She accepted. A few days later I

---

[24]The *Sea Tiger* was a weekly newspaper distributed throughout the III MAF area of northern South Vietnam, published by the III Marine Amphibious Force.

picked her up in my cool-looking white 1959 Chevrolet sports coupe. We attended the play, and afterwards, we circled the local fast-food teen hangout called The Drumstick. We ordered some of their famous batter-covered French fries and a coke. After eating and visiting, we headed back to her house to make the 10:00 p.m. curfew which we abided by up to the day we married. We had a great time on our first date, but later she told me that I had been shy and quiet. This was to be the beginning of a long and happy life together. Three years later on November 30, 1963, we were married.

As I sat on the sandbags around our bunker, day-dreaming about Marilyn, our first date, and the day I would return home, I was jarred back into reality by incoming enemy mortars. I made a dive for the entrance to our bunker as the mortars exploded around our position, destroying the sand bags we had filled and placed on top of our bunker. It was a quick reminder that I had to stay alert if I planned to return home to Marilyn and our baby.

As soon as there was a pause in the firing, we were out of our bunkers, adjusting our mortars and firing towards the enemy positions. The exact location of the enemy was a guessing game because we were unable to see the direction or know the distance of their firing. We only had an approximate idea of where they were, so we fired in that direction until their firing stopped, letting us know we must have hit their position.

First platoon from our company was sent out to check on the enemy site; they discovered we had been on target. They found the enemy had evacuated, leaving bloody drag marks from their dead and wounded. It felt like we were in a cat-and-mouse game, because the NVA and VC were good at hiding and moving without being detected. By the time we thought we had located them, they had moved on to a new location. For the next few days, we focused on packing up our gear and weapons. We had orders to move back to Dong Ha and then on to Camp Evans.

A woman giving birth to a child
has pain because her time has come; but when
her baby is born she forgets the anguish because of her joy
that a child is born into the world.
(John 16:21 NIV)

DERL HORN

Marilyn: Derl and I both entered the month of November with excitement, knowing we were only weeks away from the birth of our first baby. I was apprehensive with the unknown of labor and delivery; all of this was made more difficult without Derl. Mother and Dad were attentive, supportive, and encouraging as they understood it was a hard time for me. The morning of November 21st, I woke up with back pain as Mother was getting ready for work, but I didn't really think much about it. As the morning progressed, I felt the pain getting stronger, but doubted myself, not really knowing what it was like to have a contraction. By midmorning I decided to walk across the street and get the opinion of our neighbor, Betty Davis, a registered nurse. I explained what was happening and my uncertainty about what to do. She began to time the contractions as she felt each one and insisted that I call the doctor. Dr. Mashburn told me to meet him at the hospital, so I called Mother to let her know she would need to take off work.

At around five p.m., to our shock and surprise, I delivered two baby girls, weighing five pounds, seven ounces, and three pounds, seven ounces. I had been given a drug that made me sleep, so I was unaware of what had taken place. Around seven that evening, two young nurses' aids told me I had given birth to twin girls. Not believing my ears, I began to cry. My first thoughts were Are they healthy? and How am I ever going to manage two babies?

It wasn't long before Mother and Dad were in the room, reassuring me that I would be fine and they would help me take care of the babies. It was hard to process the news. I had two babies, not just one. I was full of gratitude, but the element of fear stood in the shadows. I refused to allow the fear to rob me of the joy of these two beautiful baby girls, Cynthia Carolyn and Nancy Catherine Horn.

Early the next morning, I was wheeled down the hall in a wheelchair to see the girls lying together in an incubator. They were so tiny it scared me, but the doctor assured me they were healthy and would be fine. In a few hours I was able to hold Cindy, but it would be four weeks before I could hold Cathy. Family and friends were flooding my room with flowers, gifts, and offers to help.

I was unaware but this was a very special day as Marilyn gave birth to our twin daughters around 1700 hours at Washington Regional Hospital in Fayetteville. In my letters I told her I was anxious to hear from her. I let her know how much I loved her and missed her and how hard it was to wait for November 26th, the due date of our baby. I thanked her for sending me another tape-recorded message. It reassured me to hear her voice even though it left me feeling sad and homesick. I received three packages of goodies in the mail, one from Marilyn, one from my sister Norma, and one from our friends Sharon and Dee Spann. I let them all know in a letter that my buddies and I were thoroughly enjoying the goodies and to please keep them coming.

At Con Thien our company was being replaced by 1st Battalion, 1st Marine Regiment, 1st Marine Division. We were privileged to ride in a convoy instead of walking from Con Thien back to Dong Ha. Unfortunately we didn't make it back to Dong Ha in time for a shower, even though we all needed one. I had not been able to shower for the month we were at Con Thien.

After lunch the next day I held a weapons inspection for my men, and they all passed. The inspections in Vietnam were different from those in the States. There was no spit and shine. Our main concern was to be certain our weapons were functional. We also had pay call. I was one of the lucky ones to receive my money. I sent $299.00 home to Marilyn and kept $30.00 for miscellaneous spending. I still had $300.00 on the books that I was saving for my R&R in Hong Kong in December.

We were issued two more mortars, bringing us up to three mortar squads. We barely had enough men to staff the mortars, and I was stretched thin with the responsibility of being squad leader and section leader. We continued to hope that more men would join us soon.

The long-awaited day for showers finally arrived, and it felt good to wash off the layers of dirt. I must have soaped up a dozen times. I remember thinking, *When I get home I plan to soak in a tub for hours with my sweetheart washing my back.* I was enjoying the goodies from home, especially the candles Marilyn sent that we used to light up the inside of our bunker. The pens and paper she sent were used to write letters home. The cigarettes in my box were a rare treat. I was anxious to take pictures with the film Marilyn had sent. I wanted her and my family to see my friends, our bunkers, and the countryside so they would have an idea of what life was like in Vietnam. I hoped that by the time she received my letter, she would be holding little Cindy or Chris. I couldn't wait for pictures of her and our baby. I knew she would be a loving mother and take good care of our little one.

We celebrated Thanksgiving with a church service, but we kept on guard, always attentive for the sounds of mortar and rocket rounds. Later in the day we were transferred by helicopter to Nam

Hoa, better known to Marines as "The Rock Crusher." The Seabees crushed rocks from the mountain to make gravel.[25] It was to be used to build roads and for construction in other locations, even though I hadn't seen any roads being built in the area. The choppers brought us into the landing zone and hovered, allowing us time to jump out. The choppers tried not to stay in one place very long because they always drew mortar and rocket fire. We jumped from the choppers with our mortars and full gear, making for an awkward and hard landing. We rolled as we landed, then gathered up our gear and ran for cover as mortar rounds exploded all around us. They were attempting to shoot down the chopper and kill Marines, but we managed to escape without injury, and the chopper lifted off safely. Our mission at the "Rock Crusher" was to provide security for the Seabees as they worked with their trucks and heavy equipment. The mountain reminded me of our mountains back home in Arkansas. This one was steep enough to make you want to stay put after you managed to climb to the top.

    I positioned one of our 60mm mortar squads down by the river at the bottom of the mountain to guard the ferryboat that transferred gravel trucks back and forth across the river. I placed the second mortar at the bottom on the other side of the mountain and my squad on top of the mountain, giving us a good view for miles around. I plotted out the areas to fire each of the mortars, and we immediately began firing H-and-I rounds into the suspected VC positions.[26] We continued to do so daily. We were fortunate to have some wooden hardback buildings at this location and even had a mess hall, but unfortunately these were all at the bottom of the mountain. It was a thirty-minute hike down the mountain and then another steep hike back up, so our squad chose to eat C-rations for most of our meals.

    The special day finally arrived, November 26th, the date our baby was due to enter into the world and for me to become a daddy. So far I had not received word from Marilyn, so I assumed that we

---

[25] A Seabee is a member of the United States Navy Construction Battalion (CB). The word "Seabee" comes from initials "CB." The Seabees have a history of building bases, bulldozing and paving thousands of miles of roadway and airstrips, and accomplishing a myriad of other construction projects in a wide variety of military theaters dating back to World War II. From Wikipedia, the free encyclopedia

[26] Harassment and Interdiction missions entailed firing on known enemy trails, hang-outs, etc. at random times to keep the enemy off balance. ARTILLERY TERMS AND TACTICS

were still waiting. The Red Cross was to send me a message when our baby arrived. I was nervous and anxious, thinking about Marilyn, wondering about the delivery and whether Marilyn and our baby were okay. The homesickness was hard to manage, as I really wanted to be at home to share in the birth and to help Marilyn care for our little one. It was hard not to worry, since I didn't know what was happening. All I could think was, *Is she in the hospital? Has the baby arrived?* and *Are they both healthy?* Waiting without any communication from her or her parents was very difficult, but I was hopeful to hear something soon.

I stayed busy plotting our firing concentration areas on the map for all three squads and training the men to plot their own concentration. It was hard and time consuming for me to hike down and back up the mountain so many times a day. As new Marines were added to our mortar section, the training continued so these new men could learn to be an effective part of their new squad. I wanted to be sure the squad leaders were well-trained and familiar with plotting and running their squads before I left for home in two-and-a-half months.

The relentless monsoon rains continued to pour day and night with no relief in sight. The weather continued to be hot and humid, but we managed to get our daily firing missions accomplished. We attempted to dry out in our bunker during the time we had between firing missions.

The bulk of the firing took place during the night hours, as we tried to ward off the NVA and VC from setting up new positions. New Marines continued to be assigned to our company, making us only four men short of having a full mortar section. It felt good to have three squads, even though most of these men were new and needed training along with experience in how to respond during battle. The whole time I had been in Vietnam, we had worked to rebuild Bravo Company. I had joined the company as a replacement only a month before the July 2nd battle when we lost all but twenty-six Marines out of our company of 150. It had been a constant struggle to regroup and rebuild, leaving us with very few seasoned Marines. That was a dangerous position for us

John Gunning, Ronnie Fields, unknown, Tom Hines

Back Home

My in-laws, Tom & Neva Buchanan
Kenneth and Tom Buchanan Jr.

Marilyn with brother
Kenneth Buchanan

24

OUR WEDDING ANNIVERSARY

On November 30, 1967, Marilyn and I celebrated our fourth year of marriage. Thanks to Uncle Sam we had been separated for two out of the four years, but the old saying, "absence makes the heart grow fonder," was especially true in our case. The first two years together, we celebrated by going out for a steak dinner and a movie. The third anniversary found me in Cuba, and for our fourth anniversary, I was in the God-forsaken place called Vietnam. It was fun to anticipate the celebration of our next anniversary when I would be home in Arkansas or wherever a job would take us. At the moment, my heart was heavy and my thoughts took me back to Marilyn and our wedding day. I missed her so much and wished I could be home. I knew she would be thinking about me and all the wonderful times we had together. We had spent the first years of marriage getting to know each other and having many fun experiences as a couple. Now our family of two was about to change with a baby on its way.

I will never forget the night I asked Marilyn to marry me. I was so excited but really nervous. After returning her home from a date, I managed to work up the courage to ask her to marry me, and I was surprised with her quick response of yes. The next step was the hardest part—asking her parents' permission. I will never forget that evening as most of her family was home, visiting in the living room. I was sitting there, trying to work up the courage to ask her parents for permission when Marilyn's younger brother, Kenneth, blurted out that we had something to ask them. I assume at some point he had overheard us talking about marriage, as he seemed to always be hiding and spying on us when we were home. One evening, while we were sitting on the couch, we noticed movement behind us. He was outside, jumping up to look in the picture window, trying to catch us kissing. No need for a chaperone when you have a little brother.

Finally, I gained the courage to ask her parents the question: "Could we get married?" After they listened very attentively to me, her dad gave us his permission and blessing. However, shortly after the conversation, her mom jumped up and said, "I think I smell something burning in the kitchen." She exited, never to return that night. I could see she was upset. Years later, I would better understand the disappointment of dreams we have for our children. Her dream was for Marilyn to finish college before marriage. Our plan was for Marilyn to continue at the university, but we didn't want to wait three more years for her to graduate. We also thought marriage might delay my draft notice.

A few weeks before the wedding, Marilyn's mom had a serious talk with her about how marriage was a lifetime commitment and making a wedding vow before God was a serious issue. She emphasized that divorce was not an option, and we would have to resolve any problems between us. Marilyn would not be allowed to run back home. That conversation caused some tears, but I reassured Marilyn that her mom was only trying to help her see the seriousness of marriage.

That spring Marilyn finished her first year of college at the University of Arkansas. Then in the summer she worked to save money for the wedding and stayed busy making plans. Her mom was still not enthusiastic about planning the wedding, so her dad called for a family meeting. He told Marilyn's mom that we were going to have a wedding and she could choose to either be a part or not, but either way the marriage was taking place. He said that she could help plan a church wedding, or we would have a private ceremony. She reluctantly agreed to help us. She only wanted us to wait until Marilyn finished with college. After we returned from our honeymoon, Marilyn's parents treated me like a son. They were supportive, loving, and kind throughout the years. They were Godly parents, in-laws, and grandparents. And when the day came, they welcomed Marilyn back home while I was deployed to Cuba and Vietnam.

My Girls

Marilyn holding Cynthia on left and Cathy on right

Cindy left, Cathy right, five and half month old

25

TWIN DAUGHTERS

On December 3, 1967 at 14:30 hours, I received an urgent call from the Command Post to come down as soon as possible. I hurried off my mountain-top position on the "Rock Crusher," expecting to hear about a problem with one of the mortar positions. When I arrived, I was handed the radio phone. The operator on the other end identified himself as being with the Red Cross and told me that my wife and daughters were fine. I was in shock as I held the radio phone, thinking about what I had just heard.

The man said, "Corporal Horn, are you still there?"

I replied, "Yes sir, I thought you said daughters as in plural."

He replied, "Yes, I did. You are the father of twin girls, and your wife and daughters are fine."

I could not believe what I was hearing and said, "You are kidding me, right?" He started apologizing about not notifying me sooner. Our twins were born on Tuesday, November 21st, at 5:30 p.m., but he said that they had been unable to locate me. My company had moved from Con Thien to Dong Ha to Camp Evans, and then to Nam Hoa in just a couple of weeks. Unfortunately, the timing of those moves had made it hard for the Red Cross to track me down.

I finally realized that this man was not kidding and I was truly the father of twin girls. He told me that my father-in-law had been working with the Red Cross, trying to locate me. He was not happy with a twelve-day delay. Marilyn had been upset and crying over the lack of communication about our babies. When her dad saw how upset she was, he took matters into his own hands and went to the Red Cross. He left early on a Saturday morning for the Red Cross office and demanded a response back from me by the next day. Amazingly they were able to accomplish this, as the telegram arrived on Sunday morning. The Red Cross representative called Marilyn on Sunday morning and read the message they had received from me, then he put the telegram in the mail the next day.

The news of the twins seemed unreal to me. It was hard for me to believe we had grown from a family of two to a family of four. I had two babies almost two weeks old, and I was just now finding it out. I was relieved and thankful to God for my wife and healthy babies.

Marilyn: *The next few weeks were the normal adjustment for a new mother and baby with one exception—the daddy did not know they had arrived. With each letter I received, Derl was agonizing with concern about the baby arrival, knowing I was past due for delivery. I was frustrated that he had not been contacted by the Red Cross. By the end of the second week, I was heartsick because everyone knew but Derl and I began to cry. As my dad passed my bedroom, he saw how upset I was. He said, "Twelve days has been long enough. I am headed to the Red Cross office in Fayetteville to get answers." The next day around noon, the Red Cross called to read me a telegram that they had received, giving Derl's response to the news of the births. I was relieved that he finally knew his babies had arrived.*

That evening after the phone call about the twins, I received a letter during mail call from Marilyn's mom, telling me about the birth and how Marilyn was doing. Had I not received the phone call, I would have been informed by Mom's letter. She shared how excited our family and friends were and that the twins looked like their mother with blond hair and blue eyes. She said the doctor was shocked that she had twins since she had only gained fifteen pounds during the pregnancy. Mom assured me that the babies and Marilyn were healthy and doing well. She included pictures and the newspaper clipping of their birth. Marilyn used the name we had picked out for our girl for the first-born baby, Cynthia Carolyn. Then she and her parents named the second twin also after her sister, naming her Nancy Catherine. Both girls were given part of her sister's name, Nancy Carolyn Buchanan Gettig, who was killed in a tragic head-on car accident three years earlier. The other names were chosen from great-grandparents. The following day, I received several more letters from home, including one from Marilyn with pictures of her and our babies. They were beautiful. Marilyn's dad included a box of cigars that I shared with my friends. We had a puffing good time with the "It's a girl" cigars. The enemy probably thought the mountain was on fire.

December 4. Just when I thought it could not get any better than having twins, I was notified that I would be going to Hong Kong for my R&R on December 16 through the 24th. At first I thought I might spend Christmas in Hong Kong, but that did not happen. It did not matter. I was just happy to be going for a break.

We stayed busy on the mountain, humping ammo up to our top position and then firing our mortars with H-&-Is at night to keep the enemy around us from organizing an attack on our positions. It continued to rain almost every day; when it was not raining, the heat and humidity made it difficult to breathe. We were on watch around the clock, as we protected the Seabees while they collected and ground up rocks. We continued to get sporadic incoming mortars and rockets, along with sniper fire that sent bullets screaming around our ears like mad bees. We were getting incoming mortars and small arms fire from areas that required permission to fire back because it was in a No Fire Zone. By the time we received permission to fire, the VC had moved to another location, dropping more mortar rounds again on our position. They managed to get a lucky hit that knocked out a hilltop observation bunker, which happened to be empty at the time. It was a crazy war!

26

ROCK APE AMBUSH

At 18:30 hours as we finished up our first round of H-&-I mortar firing and gathered inside our bunker for the night assignments, we heard several thumps against the bunker that sounded like grenades. We hit the deck but no explosions followed. As we cautiously crawled from our bunker with our weapons, another barrage hit our bunkers. After closer inspection, we realized that someone was throwing rocks at us. First, we thought it could be some of the other Marines playing a joke, but then we thought they would know that would be too risky and could get someone killed. After further observations, we could see a form around the clefts outside our perimeter. It was just dark enough that we could not make out what it was, but finally we decided that it must be the rock apes we had heard other Marines talk about. We were told that these apes were reddish-brown in color, stood four to five feet tall, and walked mostly upright. Whatever they were, they were accurate at throwing rocks. They were fairly harmless unless you happened to be the target of one of their rocks. They stayed at a distance and would disappear into the bushes or behind boulders when we looked for them. I guess they did not like us very much and threw rocks to let us know, or maybe they were just hoping to scare us away. Vietnam was a crazy place.

During the day, we went on search-and-destroy patrols, but the VC knew how to stay hidden. We were not finding much other than old bunkers and trenches where they had dug positions to fire on our mountain. We continued to fire mortars into likely enemy locations as we kept looking for them, but without much luck. It was still wet and mucky, and the rain just kept coming. We were a bunch of drenched Marines as we waded through overflowing trenches and rice paddies up to our waists. Our canteens were empty, so we had to use water from streams near the rice paddies. I kept wondering what was in that water. I know human fertilizer was used on the rice paddies, and the rain caused the paddies to overflow into the streams. Thank God for Kool-Aid to make the water taste better and Halazone tabs to kill the germs and some of the bad taste.

Some mornings on the hill, we had requests for quick fire missions because the enemy threats were nearby. During those times we fired the mortar without the bipod, just holding it and adjusting the tube by hand. This was a quick way, but not very accurate. After a few rounds the tube would get too hot to handle.

There were times when we felt the need to be extra careful. Those times were when we had a rotation date out of Vietnam and back to the States, or when we were issued a time for going on R&R. Both of those dates were fast approaching for me.

27

LETTER FROM
LIEUTENANT COLONEL J. F. MITCHELL

Back home, Marilyn got a Christmas greeting letter from the Commanding Officer of 1st Battalion, 9th Marines, 3rd Marine Division, written on December 10th.

Dear Family of a Marine of the 1st Battalion, 9th Marines,

My most sincere greeting to all of the loved ones at home from all of us of the 1st Officer of this Battalion and with the concurrence of the officers and men, that I communicate with you and express our feelings as the holiday season approaches. You have given us the finest men that this Battalion, and the Marine Corps, has ever had. That you are concerned about us is evident from the many letters we receive and the varied assorted packages that you send. That you have a lot invested in us is evident, as I take proud notice of the dedicated husbands and sons you have sent.

Please let me try to tell you how important you really are. Each and every man in the Marines has a very important two-fold job to accomplish while he is here. One part of that job is to win this war. Many times we are reminded of the importance of this job when we experience the personal dangers inherent in this war. Many times we thank God that we are able to fight this war so that you, our loved ones will be spared the frustrations, mental and physical anguish that war brings. Our "Native Land" has been spared this for many years. These Marines of yours are giving their best so that lasting peace, where you live, will continue.

Secondly, each man has another important job; coming back to you when his tour is finished. To this end, be assured that every bit of his energy, professional skill and talent are being put forth. In this light, your moral support by your encouraging letters and reports concerning his loved ones and his home, give him the peace of mind so necessary for him to continue his winning ways. Please continue this very vital help with your letters of encouragement.

On Thanksgiving Day, we gathered in Church Services and we thanked God for many things. We thanked Him for life, safety and for those who have died so that we might live; we are indeed, humbly grateful. We also thanked Him for you who have given so much, as we prayed for your safety and health back home.

This Battalion has had an impressive share of the load in fighting this war. I thought you would like to know that in every instance its members have accredited themselves to the highest degree. Their valor, dedication, devotion to duty and country, will be one of my most cherished memories. You can be justly proud of them. This letter comes to you at a joyous time in the year. When we think about all of you, home and the holiday season, we wish we were with you. But by continuing to do our job we know that we are making it possible for us to be together in future holiday seasons. We want you to share these thoughts and to join in this hope for the future.

In the name of all of us in the 1st Battalion, 9th Marines, I wish you every blessing of this season knowing that the New Year of 1968 will find us still free, still giving so much that others might have freedom, full of peace and Thanksgiving.

Very Truly Yours,
JF Mitchell
Lieutenant Colonel,
U. S. Marine Corps Commanding Officer

28

R & R IN HONG KONG

December 13. The time had finally arrived for me to begin making my way out of the country for R&R in Hong Kong. As my company was moving toward Hill 51 near Camp Evans, I was able to catch a convoy headed to Phu Bia where we had a 1st Battalion, 9th Marine transit facility. I spent the night there and then caught another convoy going on to Camp Evans the next day. After arriving at Camp Evans, I picked up my travel orders and then exchanged most of my gear for civilian clothes for my trip. Catching another convoy, I headed back to Phu Bia to turn in my rifle, ammo, flak jacket, and helmet. I went to the dispersing office to draw out the money I had on the books, amounting to $485.00. At the air terminal, I caught a flight on a C-130 to Da Nang. Arriving late, I found the R&R center filled to capacity, so I was issued a cot to use in the air terminal for the night. I didn't complain because it was more comfortable than sleeping on the ground. The next day after receiving three required immunizations for travel to Hong Kong, I was sent to another building and assigned a bunk bed, mattress, sheets and blankets for the night. After a long shower, I crawled between the sheets for a good night's sleep. It felt good to be clean and in a real bed. Next to my cot was another Marine on his way to Australia for R&R. We chatted for a little bit about how happy we were to be away from the war for a while. Both of us were married and anxious to get home to our wives, but for the moment, we were relaxed and enjoyed being away. The next morning we attended a required lecture on the do's and don'ts while on leave. We were warned against being AWOL by being late or failing to catch our flight back to Vietnam. A few hours later I caught a commercial flight out of Da Nang around 1500 hours, headed for Hong Kong.

The flight was smooth and right on schedule. When we arrived in Hong Kong, a bus was waiting to transport us to the Empress Hotel on Chatham Road in Kowloon, Hong Kong. My room turned out to be on the seventh floor, room number 704. It was much nicer than I had expected. Back home it would have been an expensive stay, but there I had five nights for only $35.00. Checking in at the hotel, I didn't see many of the other soldiers and Marines who had flown over with me. Most of them were young unmarried men, already off to spend most of their time and money on women in bars and night clubs.

The first thing I wanted to do was call home and talk with my sweet wife. I couldn't wait to hear her voice after many months of separation. I could hardly wait to hear what she was doing and the latest news about our baby girls. I was anxious to tell her how much I loved her and to let her know I was counting down the days until I would see her in February, if not before. Our conversation had to be short since it was very costly to make an international call. The phone call was the highlight of my trip to Hong Kong. I heard the voice of my sweetheart and the sounds of Cindy crying. It made it real…I was a dad!

Cindy was not yet a month old. I couldn't touch her or see her, but I could hear her cry. Cathy was still in the Washington Regional Medical Hospital, growing and gaining weight so she could come home soon. I was excited to only have two months left in the Marines. I knew the day was coming when we would finally be together again and this nightmare would be over. Knowing I was so close to going home made the waiting harder. After our phone visit it was difficult to say good-bye.

Marilyn: *After the birth of Cindy and Cathy, the days quickly flew by with the demands of caring for two tiny infants. There were never enough hours in the day. Caring for Cindy at home and making trips to the hospital to see Cathy kept us all busy. One morning in mid-December, the phone rang. I picked it up* *to hear the sweetest voice. Derl was calling me from Hong Kong! He had arrived for his R&R, settled into his hotel, and was anxious to visit. His voice had never sounded better. There was so much I wanted to tell him, and yet I couldn't think of a thing because I was so excited. His questions were about me and the babies and what was happening at home. Cathy was still in the hospital, but I quickly ran to pick up Cindy who was sleeping and brought her to the phone. I tried to arouse her, but she wouldn't wake up so I gently pinched her leg (I'm sorry, Cindy). She then began to cry, letting Daddy hear her voice. He could not believe he was hearing his baby. The call was short and sweet, but hearing my sweetheart's voice was the best Christmas gift ever!*

After the phone call, I was ready to explore the city and find a place to eat. I looked forward to some good food after months of eating C-rations. I ended up eating a good-looking sandwich and some noodles in a small cafe. With my hunger satisfied, I began looking for a tailor shop to fit me for a new suit. I found a place called Handsome Tailor at the Empress Hotel on Chatham Road. Astor Chang, the tailor, helped me choose the fabric. Mr. Chang took my measurements and gave me a time to return for a fitting. I was excited to think about the day I would wear my suit to church with my wife and family. Feeling good about the material selection, my next mission was to find gifts for my family. I wanted something special for each one.

I shopped in many of the stores in the downtown area. I was looking for pearl necklaces and finally purchased three strands of pearls after haggling over the price with the salesman. He wanted $35 for each necklace, but he finally agreed to let me purchased them for $14.50 each. The pearls were gifts for my mom and mother-in-law and a good family friend. I purchased two watches, one for my father-in-law and one for myself for a total of $25. Marilyn wanted a hairpiece to wear for special occasions. I found one that I thought was close to her hair color for $65HKD (Hong Kong dollars), only $3.75 in American dollars.

I had looked forward to my time in Hong Kong for many months, but now I realized how quickly the days were passing. I was due to leave at 7:15 a.m. on December 21st. It was difficult to believe that I was in Hong Kong, living like a civilian and even looking like one. It felt good to relax, knowing that no one was trying to kill me.

How I longed to live this way again, to feel safe. My only issues since arriving in Hong Kong were the awful bad dreams that woke me up during the night. These images were so real, making me feel like I was still under fire in Vietnam. It took several minutes after I woke up to realize that I was in a safe place.

A few days later, I picked up my new suit from the tailor and wore it to dinner at a hotel where I enjoyed a delicious steak while listening to a band play Christmas Carols. The music brought back such warm memories of home, causing waves of homesickness. It made me want to forget all I had been through and just take the next flight back to Arkansas. Instead, I went to my hotel room and took another long, hot, relaxing bath. After being refreshed and relaxed, I lay down for a few minutes; before I knew it I was asleep. When morning had arrived, I was disappointed that I had missed the sightseeing plans I had made for the evening on the town. I didn't realize how much I needed the sleep.

On Monday, December 18th, I awoke rested and ready to have some fun. I bought three tickets for sightseeing tours costing $3.75 American dollars. The Hong Kong dollar exchange was only worth $.18 to the American dollar at that time. My first stop was a Hong Kong island tour. For lunch, we stopped at a very nice Malaysian restaurant where we enjoyed shrimp, rice, sweet and sour beef. The food was good, and trying to eat with chopsticks gave me a good workout. Our meal concluded with a free drink, so I had a Tom Collins.

There were fourteen of us on the tour, including two couples on their way back to the States from Thailand. They questioned me about my family and seemed interested in hearing about our twin daughters waiting for me at home. One of the ladies was an Australian Women's Army Corps (WAC); the other was an Australian soldier who had also been drafted. The rest of the men were soldiers or Marines from Vietnam. The tour took us through a very poor area of the city near the immigration housing. We stopped at an open-air market crowded with people. Our guide warned us to be careful and watch our wallets because of the many thieves and pickpockets. At the market, we watched a man skin a snake and then sell the meat to his customers. The guide said he had eaten snake before and it tasted terrible. I believed him and did not try any.

Our next stop was a swanky nightclub where we watched a floor show as we sipped more drinks. We were entertained with a Chinese opera titled "Madam Butterfly." The tour guide tried to explain the story line to us as the colorful, costumed Chinese actors darted about the stage, singing and dancing. I had a hard time following the plot, but it was amusing to watch. After the opera we concluded the tour by visiting Juno, a revolving restaurant twenty-five stories high. It provided a fantastic view of the city. We enjoyed the view as well as the wonderful food. The tour concluded around 12:30 a.m. and returned us to our hotel. I returned to my room feeling dizzy and nauseous, thinking I had too many drinks. I then remembered how shrimp had made me sick on the Marine Corps birthday at Con Thien, realizing I had thoughtlessly eaten shrimp again. The bed felt good, and even though the room seemed to be spinning around me, I managed to quickly fall into a deep sleep.

The next morning I had another tour planned for 9:30 a.m., but I overslept until 11:00 a.m. I had to reschedule this tour for my last day. My time was passing much faster than it did in the fields of Vietnam. I finished my shopping, buying a Kodak Super 8 movie camera and projector to send home along with some cute handmade baby clothes for our little girls.

I enjoyed wearing my new tailor-made suit around town. I felt sharp. A young Chinese boy hung around me almost everywhere I went, trying to sell me his virgin sister or his virgin mother. He obviously did not understand the meaning of the word *virgin*. It was sad to see and hear what these children had to do for money. I had no interest in his family, but I did allow him to take some movies of me walking down the streets of Hong Kong. I wanted Marilyn to have the movies of me in my new suit and to see Hong Kong. I was fortunate the young boy didn't run off with my new camera. He seemed like a good kid just trying to make money the only way he knew how.

On my last day in Hong Kong I took an island tour that turned out to be a very interesting experience. Crossing the harbor by ferry, we proceeded to the top of Victoria Peak by trolley for a breathtaking panoramic view of the metropolis below. We traveled by bus to Tiger Balm Gardens, a fantasy land of sculptured figures. We then wound our way through Happy Valley and on to Deep Water Bay and

Aberdeen, home of Hong Kong's numerous floating populations. This group of people lived on the water, making fishing and transporting people their livelihood. Most of them were born on the boats, raised their families there, and died on their boats. We divided up the group and boarded individual sampans that rowed us out to Sea Palace, The Floating Restaurant to have lunch. On the deck of the restaurant, each of us chose our meal from the large tubs filled with live fish. After we made our selection, the fish was removed from the tub and prepared for our meal with all the trimmings. The food was great, and it was a fun experience, but I could not keep from thinking about Marilyn and our two precious baby girls back home. I was again feeling homesick for them and dreaded going back to the fields of Vietnam. But I had my tour of duty to finish.

December 21. The next morning all of the Marines and soldiers returning from leave were bused back to the airport to catch a 7:15 a.m. flight back to Vietnam. We landed in Da Nang and were sent to the R&R center. I had planned to stop in An Hoa the following day to visit with my brother-in-law, Kenneth. I was disappointed when I realized it would be impossible since there were no choppers headed that way and I was still without my weapons. I was able to visit with a Marine who had served with me at Camp Lejeune and another one who served with me in Cuba. We chatted for a few minutes before I met up with Richard Hosey, a buddy from Mississippi. I had met him in Okinawa while waiting for our flights to Vietnam. We reminisced about our time in Okinawa, shared some of our experiences in Vietnam, then had some pictures taken together to send home. Richard was just beginning his leave to Hong Kong and mine was over. It seemed a shame that we didn't get to spend our time together in Hong Kong for a good time together. I will never forget Richard telling me that I looked more like a family man than a military person, and I should be home with my family instead of fighting in Vietnam. It wasn't hard to agree with him since I longed to be home with my wife and daughters, but that would not happen for another two months. Later I was thankful to hear that Richard returned safely to his hometown about five months after I saw him. He still lives in Mississippi with his wife, kids, and grandkids. We stay in touch with an occasional phone call or e-mail.

That evening, I bunked at the R&R Center and woke up the next morning to find that some low scum had lifted my wallet and pictures of my lovely wife and beautiful daughters. I was sick and mad that someone would stoop so low. It was a good thing that I did not know who it was. I remembered just before going to sleep that I had looked at my pictures and placed them in an envelope and put them in my pocket. I guess whoever saw me do this thought it was money. I did have $35.00 in my wallet that they took but fortunately I had my I.D. and orders in a separate place. Right away I wrote Marilyn, asking her to send me new pictures as soon as possible. I was looking forward to getting back to the base so I could pick up the mail I had missed over the past ten days.

I boarded a C130 out of Da Nang to Phu Bia where I spent the night and enjoyed watching a couple of movies, *The Wild, Wild West* and *Bonanza*. They were a good distraction from my thoughts of Vietnam and what I was headed back to. I caught a convoy back to Camp Evans where I then reported back to duty on December 24th around noon. I was asking myself, *Could this really be Christmas Eve?*

All my thoughts were instantly centered on home where I imagined myself enjoying my wife and family and eating turkey and dressing with all the trimmings. For dessert, I would be having a large piece of Karo nut pie, or pecan pie as some call it, my absolute favorite. The women in my family—my mom, Marilyn's mom and Marilyn—were experts on making a delicious pecan pie. It was hard to think about being so far from home. The song "I'll Be Home for Christmas" described it well for me; in my dreams, I was truly home.

After I had checked in, I picked up my mail and was overjoyed to find nine letters from Marilyn, Christmas cards, letters and packages from my mom, my dad, and my brother-in-law Kenneth. Kenneth was also serving in Vietnam with Golf Company of the 2nd Battalion, 5th Marines, 1st Marine Division. There were also Christmas cards and gifts from friends: Sharon and Dee Spann, Jackie and Sam Wilson, my Aunt Stella, and Ron Kist, another buddy serving in Vietnam. I also heard from my younger sis, Myra, and her husband Bill DeVault; my older sister, Norma, and her husband Dale Eastburn; my cousins Pat and Neil Broadhead; friends Oddy and Sandy Straight; Gene McCulley; H.A. Test; Mr. and Mrs. D.O. Smith; Paula and Randy Smith; Troy, Marie and Max Ryan; Olive Miller; Margaret and Bill Johnson; Landreth and Jimmie Loyd; Tracy and

June Barrett; Norman and Ruth Marie Crowder; and Mrs. H.R. Sharp. It felt wonderful to have so many family and friends thinking about me and looking forward to my return. Those letters and cards encouraged me and made for a better Christmas Eve.

29
MERRY CHRISTMAS IN VIETNAM

December 25, 1967. Christmas was another lonely day. The year before I spent Christmas in Cuba, guarding the dividing fence between Cuba and Gitmo Bay. I had hoped and prayed that I would spend this Christmas with my wife and family. I was consumed with thoughts about home and family. The best Christmas gift I received was a letter from my sweet wife, along with a package containing a Bible, pens and goodies. I was thankful for each gift I received, including a letter from mother, two cartons of cigarettes, and stationery from Dad.

I attended a Christmas church service under a tent full of shrapnel holes. The Christmas message was a reassuring reminder that Jesus Christ had come into this world to seek and to save the lost, to offer the free gift of eternal life and heaven to those who believed in Him. I was thankful for the assurance of knowing I had placed my faith in Christ. Regardless of what happened in this war zone, I would one day be in heaven with Him.

Christmas day was full of surprises, one being a visit from the USMC Career Adviser. He offered to give me an extension package in the Marine Corps. This would include extra pay and a promotion to sergeant, with a new stripe. He was practically begging me to sign on the dotted line. My comment was, "You are talking to me in the wrong place, at the wrong time." I was ready to be home with my family.

In the afternoon I enjoyed watching a movie, then eating Christmas dinner served with free sodas. The coke turned out to be my favorite item. It tasted so good. All in all, it was about the best Christmas a combat Marine could hope for in Vietnam. I felt sorry for my buddies who were out on Hill 51 eating C-rations or whatever they could find to eat.

I remained at Camp Evans for two more days, waiting to catch a chopper out to Hill 51. I didn't complain about the delay. It was a relief not to have someone shooting at me. My only assignment was standing guard duty and being on alert, so my time there was quiet and restful. The one exception was when a Marine intentionally shot himself in the foot because he couldn't take the pressure any longer. He opted for the injury to himself, along with a dishonorable discharge from the Marine Corps. Several guys had joked about doing this, but it was hard to believe someone had actually done it.

My time was getting short for in-country, and I was very homesick. In my mind I was continually replaying my phone conversation with Marilyn while in Hong Kong. It had been wonderful to hear her voice and to hear Cindy's little, shrill cry. Cathy was still in the hospital, growing and gaining weight. She had to weigh five pounds before going home, which ended up taking another two weeks.

Marilyn: *A few days before Christmas I received a phone call from Dr. Burnside, our pediatrician, letting me know that he was releasing Cathy from the hospital. We were thrilled to know that she would be home in time for Christmas. Dad wanted to take me to pick her up while mother stayed home with Cindy. When we arrived at the hospital, the nursing staff told us they were sad to see Cathy leave after having her for four weeks, but they were happy for us. We dressed her up and tucked her into a large Christmas stocking given to us by the nurses for her homecoming. She weighed only five pounds, but she was beautiful, a precious tiny bundle in that stocking. I had wondered many times during the past four weeks how I was going to manage two babies. I was about to find out.*

30

BACK TO HILL 51

January 5, 1968. After having a few days break at Camp Evans, it was time for a chopper ride back to Hill 51, located outside Camp Evans. Our mission was to use our mortars to provide security for Camp Evans. This included defending 5,000 meters of the camp perimeter and supporting the Marines as they went out on patrols and set up ambushes.

The helicopter flew us into the landing zone with the usual mortar rounds dropping in all around us. The NVA were hoping to take out the chopper. Snipers were hiding in the tree lines and began firing on us as we made our landing. I felt like a target as I jumped from the helicopter to the ground and ran for a fox hole. As I fell into the hole, I heard a Marine comment, "Welcome back from heaven to hell." After a few minutes the chopper was able to lift off. The shooting suddenly came to a halt when some Marines shot and killed the snipers. I located my mortar section and began to settle back into life in the field.

The men were anxious to hear about my trip to Hong Kong. During the following days, I shared all I had enjoyed in Hong Kong: the food, the tours, the shopping, and the relief of being in a safe place. R&R had been an enjoyable distraction from the threat of death and suffering I had experienced during the previous eight months.

Now, the most important news I had to share was that I was

officially a "short-timer," meaning my rotation date for leaving the country would be soon. This news called for some friendly harassment and teasing from my friends. They called me a "boot." Normally a "boot" is a new recruit, but they harassed me because they had more time in the Corps and in Vietnam than I had. I came back at them with my own little saying, "Boot I may be, but out of the Corps before thee." Having been drafted into the Corps, I had a two-year hitch, while most of these Marines had three to four years to serve. The teasing was all in good fun, but my leaving early was a bitter pill for them to swallow.

Marines from our 3rd platoon spotted two Marines approaching our hill from the south. We soon learned that they had been a part of an eight-man team from Division Reconnaissance. They were the only survivors after an encounter with the enemy. A helicopter was called in to pick them up and return them to their unit at Camp Evans. The bodies of the other six Marines were not recovered for two more days.

The following day Bravo Company was ordered on a search and destroy mission. After being out on the mission for about six hours, I noticed the penholder pocket of my flak jacket was empty. The penholder is where I always hung a grenade instead of a pen; it made for easy access when I needed it. I was shocked to see that the grenade was missing, but the grenade pin was still dangling from the penholder. I immediately stopped the patrol to explain the situation and to make a short search. Since we had not heard an explosion, we assumed the grenade had been a dud.[27] I was thankful that no one had been hurt and sobered to realize I could have been injured or killed along with some of our men. I was grateful for the dud and thanked God for His protection.

Later in the afternoon we began to receive sniper fire. The sniper scout team assigned to our company spotted the VC sniper in a tree. The team began firing in that direction, shredding the leaves and killing the sniper.

One Marine stepped on an explosive device planted along the trail. He was fortunate to only get shrapnel wounds in his legs. We were tired and weary from the stress of the day's events, so we began

---

[27] A bomb, shell, or explosive round that fails to detonate.

looking for a place to settle in for the night. We had not moved far along the trail when we received more sniper fire. Thankfully, no one was hit, but one Marine broke his shoulder as he sought cover from the sniper. A medevac helicopter was called in to pick up our injured and wounded men.

I was digging a two-man foxhole for myself and my mortar when I heard a chopper coming in overhead. I quickly jumped into the foxhole, wanting to be ready to give the pilot cover in case we received enemy fire. The chopper hovered overhead, and then began to make his descent. I realized it was moving toward me—it was coming right at me. The pilot gently set the chopper down right on top of my foxhole, pinning me inside with my mortar. There was no escape. I reached up and tapped on the belly of the chopper, hoping the pilot would hear me and realize I was under him. The wounded Marines were rushed out, loaded on the chopper, and flown to safety. The only damage was to the mortar, which had been knocked out of adjustment. Having such a close encounter with the helicopter was a scary experience.

We spent the night in that location and headed out early the next morning. About mid-morning, we split up into smaller groups to do land sweeps, hunting for evidence of the enemy. As we marched along, I turned to my right and stepped on a soft spot in the ground. Before I knew what was happening I was plunging into a pongee pit. These deep pits had sharp stakes at the bottom coated with poison or human body waste to cause infection and death. The moment I started falling, I knew what to expect when I hit the bottom. I tried to hold myself stiff, in an upright position, so that when I hit the pongee stakes they would penetrate my boots and feet first. As I landed, I braced for the sharp pain, but instead, the pongee stakes crumbled beneath my boots. Thank God, the stakes were rotten, dry, and brittle, having been there, possibly, since the French war. LCorp Simon Cull dropped me a rope, and with the help of others, I was pulled to safety. We were on our way again. This close call reminded me to keep a closer watch on my steps.

The next day we continued our search, capturing a Viet Cong suspect hiding in the hedgerow. He was transferred to our Regimental Headquarters for questioning. The Marine walking point was severely mangled when he stepped on a homemade explosive device.[28] As we loaded him onto a chopper for treatment, we prayed that he would survive. The following day we had a Marine KIA and a scout wounded by another homemade explosive device. Both were flown out as soon as the weather allowed a chopper to land.

The weather was now hampering our mission with severely limited visibility due to the fog and rain. The temperature dropped into the 70s, and it felt much cooler with the lower temperature. It was difficult to sleep in wet and muddy clothes. My body shook and my teeth chattered. After a few more miserable days and nights on the search and destroy mission, we finally returned to camp.

---

[28] The point man walks several meters out in front of everyone else and is likely to be the first one to encounter enemy soldiers. It is a hazardous position that requires alertness and ability to deal with unexpected attacks. Wikipedia

31

BACK TO KHE SANH

Who of you by worrying can add a single hour to his life?
(Matthew 6:27, NIV)

January 22, 1968. I only had twenty-eight days left in the Corps, and I knew I should already be out of the field. The normal procedure was to leave the fields of Vietnam and head back to the States when you were down to thirty days. I should have been on my way home, but in Vietnam the saying was "anything goes." With only a few days left, I was being very cautious, and I prayed daily that I would make it home safely. Over the many months I had been in Vietnam, I had witnessed too many men killed in the last few days of their tour, and I did not want that to be my story.

The weather was cooperating with us. The rain had stopped, and we were back to hot days and cool nights. We received new orders. Our battalion was moving to the Khe Sanh combat base. Our new mission was to establish, occupy, and defend a defensive strongpoint northwest of the Khe Sanh combat base perimeter. The choppers coming for us were filled with Vietnamese civilians evacuated from Khe Sanh to a somewhat safer location close to Hill 51. As the civilians were herded off the choppers, we were jumping aboard, loaded with all our combat gear and weapons in preparation for the battle that was raging in Khe Sanh. We were instructed to be ready to jump off the chopper and find cover as soon as we landed on the ground because the enemy was expecting us. This was not good news for a "short-timer." We weren't kidding ourselves; we knew there would most surely be casualties. As the chopper lowered, we bailed out, hit the ground, rolling and running until we found a safe place. To our surprise and relief, no shots were fired.

After arriving at Khe Sanh, we headed for our destination northwest of the combat base. This important piece of terrain was where we expected to be busy for the next few days. Our job was to dig fox holes, put up wire fences, and place minefield obstacles around the defensive perimeter. The first morning five rockets were fired into our perimeter, and in the afternoon ten rounds of 60mm mortars were fired on us. My mortar section quickly adjusted the elevation and deflection on our mortars and returned fire. We also called in artillery to help us. It was amazing that we survived the first day without casualties. On February 5th, we had twenty-two explosions from enemy 60mm mortars and twelve from 82mm mortars; we again counter-fired with our 60mm mortars. Air strikes were called in on the NVA positions that we were able to locate. We ended the day with ten Marines sustaining minor wounds, one serious enough to be evacuated. On February 6th, we received three rounds of 60mm mortars, six rounds of 82mm mortar, four recoilless rifles, and one round of a 140mm rocket into our perimeter. We counter-fired again with our 60mm mortars and called in air strikes. This attack resulted in eleven wounded Marines with three being medevaced out. At this point I was really getting nervous, wondering if I was going to survive all of these attacks. I could not understand why I was still in the field, dodging incoming rounds, watching Marines get wounded and killed daily. It was past time for me to be leaving Vietnam, and here I was in the middle of combat.

I received a letter from Marilyn informing me that my young brother-in-law, Kenneth, serving with 1st Platoon, 2nd Squad, Golf Company, 2nd Battalion, 5th Marines, 1st Marine Division had been wounded at Hue City during the Tet Offensive.[29] Later I received the

---

[29] The Tet Offensive was one of the largest military campaigns of the Vietnam War, launched on January 30, 1968 by forces of the Viet Cong and North Vietnamese Army against South Vietnam, the United States, and their allies. It was a campaign of surprise attacks against military and civilian commands and control centers throughout South Vietnam. The operations are referred to as the Tet Offensive because there was a prior agreement to "cease fire" during the Tet Lunar New Year celebrations. Both North and South Vietnam announced on national radio broadcasts that there would be a two-day cease-fire during the holiday. Nonetheless, the Communists launched an attack that began during the early morning hours of 30 January 1968, the first day Tet. In Vietnamese, the offensive is

following letter from Kenneth explaining what took place:

Kenneth Buchanan
1st Platoon, 2nd Squad, Golf Company,
2nd Battalion, 5 Marines, 1st Marine Division

On January 30th during the beginning of the Tet Offensive, our company was ordered to give relief to the surrounded Military Assistance Command Advisors, located on the banks of the Perfume River in Hue City— which we did. We then crossed the Perfume River to link up with units of the South Vietnam Army who were surrounded in the Citadel. We were crossing the Ngyuen Hoang Bridge when it came under heavy gun fire. Each meter of advance was contested by fire power from 8,000 to 10,000 soldiers from the North Vietnam Army who had taken over Hue City during the night of January 30th. We fought our way up the streets, taking shelter in building doorways and behind trees leading into the Citadel until we were pinned down from the heavy enemy fire. Using a tree for protection, I stuck my M-79 grenade launcher around the tree to fire in the direction signaled to me by a Marine across the street. I was shot through the right hand. The round also hit my M-79, knocking the trigger guard off my weapon. Since we were pinned down and could not move forward or backwards, I put a green towel around my hand and continued firing. Our commander, Captain Meadows, directed smoke grenades up the street, and we pulled our dead and wounded back out of the ambush. After sustaining five Marines killed and forty-four wounded, our company aborted the mission into the Citadel. We pulled back to the command post and set up for the night. The next day I was medevaced by helicopter to an aid station in Phu Bai, then to the hospital at Da Nang, and then to the hospital ship, the USS Repose. I went from there to the Fort Sill Army Hospital in Oklahoma for several weeks of healing and recuperation.

Kenneth later learned that Hue City was secure and back in the hands of U.S control after a month of fierce fighting. Kenneth's First Marine Division was presented the Presidential Unit Citation by the President Lyndon B. Johnson for their bravery.

---

commonly called T⃞t M⃞u Thân (Tet, year of the monkey). Military planners called it the "General Offensive and Uprising." Wikipedia

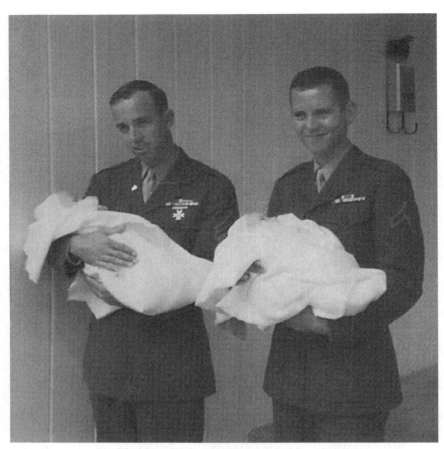
Derl holding Cathy and Kenneth holding Cindy

Kenneth Buchanan and Derl Horn

32

HEADING HOME

February 7, 1968. The big day had finally arrived. I only had seventeen days left in the Corps, and finally I received my orders for the good ol' U.S.A. My prayers had been answered, and I had survived the battlefields of Vietnam. I was thinking about home and all the good things that were waiting for me. I could hardly wait to hold my sweet-smelling wife, to again feel the softness of the woman I loved. I was excited to think about finally seeing, holding, and loving on our precious twin daughters. I was eager to hug my mom, dad, brother and sisters along with other family members and friends.

There were many things I looked forward to experiencing again: cold milk, ice cream, hamburgers, cokes, showers, a real bed, clean sheets, and riding in a car. More important, I would now feel safe, without the fear of someone trying to kill me.

There was so much ahead to look forward to, yet I realized that only another war-torn Marine could ever understand what I was feeling. It was hard for me to believe that I would no longer smell like a skunk from weeks of sweat and dirt. How good it would be to have clean shoes that were not caked with mud. So many thoughts and feelings were running through my head. I feared it would be difficult to make the adjustment back to being a normal civilian again. At that time, I had no idea how challenging it would be to cope with "normal" life. I knew there would be situations in which people back home could not understand how the war had affected me.

I said my good-byes to my Marine brothers, who were like

family to me. We had spent most of our time together in the northern part of Vietnam, close to the DMZ.

For the record, the awful reports in the newspapers and on television back home never happened, at least not to me. During my tour in Vietnam, I did not see any atrocities or experience any drug and alcohol problems. Some of the news mentioned fragging,[30] but it was neither a practice that I heard about nor one that I ever witnessed. In our company we never had Marines refuse to do their duty or refuse to follow orders. I was never aware of any racial issues. My good buddies had different skin tones— red, brown, black, and white— but it didn't matter. We were brothers, and we looked out for each other.

I left the field of battle by catching the next available chopper. After landing at the Dong Ha base, I met up with my Texas buddy, Richard Glass. We had served together in basic training at MCRD in San Diego, ITR at Camp Pendleton, extensive training in 81mm mortars at Camp Lejeune, GTMO in Cuba, and then on to Vietnam. We were separated in Vietnam and served in different outfits.

While at Camp Lejeune, I introduced Richard to Marilyn. We enjoyed having him over to our apartment for meals. We even toured the *USS North Carolina* in Wilmington together. Once, he and I stopped at the commissary to pick up groceries. As we made our selections, we noticed a Marine officer staring at us. He made us feel uncomfortable, so we hurried on to the checkout counter, paid for our groceries, and ran out the door. Later we learned we were in violation of the dress code for the commissary. We were in our work utilities when we should have been in civilian clothes or in our dress uniforms.

In Vietnam, Richard earned two Purple Hearts. While recovering from his wounds, he was assigned to light duty at a supply warehouse. After a short visit, we decided that I might want to take home a few souvenirs like new jungle boots, a poncho liner, a utility jacket, and a few other items. Richard packaged them up for me, intending to mail them to my home address, but for some unknown reason, the package never arrived. That was a blessing in disguise because I later realized I would have been stealing from our

---

[30] Killing someone using a fragmentation grenade as a weapon. *"When an American soldier killed or attempted to kill one of his superiors in Vietnam the act was called fragging because the weapon of choice, was a fragmentation grenade." Urban dictionary.*

government. After bidding Richard good-bye, I felt sad for him, knowing he still had three more months left to serve.

I caught a ride in a jeep over to the airfield where I was to catch my flight to Da Nang. There I began my journey back to the States. At the terminal I inquired about a flight and was told a chopper was headed that way, so two other Marines and I were able to board the chopper. As the pilot attempted to lift off, the chopper failed to gain altitude, leading to a crash landing. Fortunately, everyone was okay. We were told that the chopper had too many bullet holes to be flying. A bit shaken, the three of us went back inside the terminal to inquire about another flight. The officer in charge told us it was unlikely that we would fly out because of the large number of wounded Marines waiting to be evacuated. We continued to wait, hoping something would open up for us.

After about two hours, a sergeant approached us and asked if we would be willing to load some of the wounded Marines onto the C-130 that was preparing to leave. If we helped transport and care for the wounded, we would be allowed to ride out with them. We were eager to help them, so two of us picked up a wounded Marine lying on a stretcher, while the third Marine held his IV bottle. We headed for the plane, but about halfway there, mortars and rockets began falling and exploding all over the airfield. We began running with the poor Marine, determined to get on the plane even though it had already started to roll. We literally threw the man through the door and jumped in with him. As the plane left the ground, a rocket hit so close to the plane that it damaged the tail rudder, but we were already in the air. As the plane gained altitude, we turned our attention to the wounded, rejoicing that we were all finally on our way home.

We arrived at Da Nang in the early afternoon and were told to turn in our weapons and gear. Afterward we were assigned to a hut for sleeping. Early in the evening we were summoned back to headquarters and re-issued weapons. Da Nang had just been placed on a 100% alert with the threat of an attack. There was a possibility of the camp being overrun by a large number of NVA. We were assigned to an outlook trench, and I was thinking, *How could this possibly be happening again*? Did they not know that we were on our way home? How was it that we found ourselves back in the heat of battle?"

During the early morning hours, we were told the threat of the invasion was over and we could report back to our sleeping quarters. At about 0400 hours, I crawled onto a cot in a screened-in hut. Seven other Marines, also on their way home, were sleeping in the room. We had been told to report to the air terminal at 0800 hours to catch our flight to Okinawa.

I fell asleep and woke up at 0900 hours, looked around and realized everyone had left but me. I panicked, thinking I had missed my flight. Half dressed, I grabbed the rest of my clothes and bag and ran for the terminal. At the terminal I was told I would be waiting until 1300 hours for my plane to depart. As a general rule in the Marine Corps, if you are early you have to wait and if you are late, you miss out. But this time, that did not turn out to be true. I was so happy I had not missed my flight. At 1300 hours we were allowed to board the plane at last.

Finally, on February 9th, we were flying back to Okinawa. With a sigh of relief, I took one last look at the land of Vietnam, filled with all its bomb craters. In my heart, I knew I was leaving only by the grace of God. I breathed a prayer of thanksgiving, overtaken with emotion, realizing that this nightmare had finally ended.

We arrived in Okinawa, only to wait another two days before leaving for the U.S. I bumped into an old friend I had served with back in the States.

Ronald Kist, who had somehow managed to get in the Marine Corps with a bad knee and a bad eye, had just finished his tour in Vietnam. We were excited to see each other and to be on our way home. We headed over to the base club where we spent a few hours talking and sharing our experiences. Later we took in a movie as we waited for our turn to leave.

Duty in Okinawa was effortless. Okinawa civilians cleaned our barracks, made our beds, and did our laundry; the military had never been this easy. Still, I was too anxious to get home to truly enjoy the amenities.

We received our final instructions, loaded the bus, and were hauled to the airport. As we boarded the Boeing 707 on February 10th, I was again filled with relief and excitement. I thought, *Now if I can just make it across the ocean to Hawaii, then I will know that I am not just dreaming.* After we were in the air, I looked down. All I could see was water in every direction. I felt apprehensive, just as I had felt almost a year earlier, wondering if I could survive a crash into the ocean. I remembered the earlier flight over with all kinds of feelings and fears about what lay ahead of me in the war zone of Vietnam. I wondered then if I would be one of the privileged ones to return. I wanted to shout out, "Yes, I have been blessed by our Lord Jesus to return to my family!" I bowed my head in prayer to thank the Lord again for my safe return. I asked Him to help me honor all the foxhole prayers and promises that I had made to Him during my tour. It was hard to believe I was actually headed home.

After many hours in the air we landed in Hawaii for refueling. We were allowed to unload and go into the terminal for drinks and snacks. I went inside but didn't tarry long because I had come too far to be left anywhere but in Arkansas.

We landed at the El Toro Marine Corps Air Base on February 10th. As we unloaded, we were instructed to dump everything from our sea bags on a table for inspection. Anything brought from Vietnam was removed. At that point I didn't care. They could take everything I had; I just wanted to go home. It took three more days to go through the discharge process.

One day I decided to walk over to the lounge. As I walked along the road, a military truck passed by and backfired. I was in the ditch before I knew what was happening. By instinct I found a safe hole. My clean clothes were now dirty, and I was totally embarrassed. It was still hard to believe I was in the USA, ten thousand miles away from the Vietnam War.

I was happy to leave that war behind me; a war that started on September 26, 1959 and dragged on until April 30, 1975. There were 2.5 million Americans who served in Vietnam, one third as volunteers. Approximately one million were wounded, requiring medical care at the nearest hospital. In Vietnam, it took about an hour to transfer a wounded person from the battlefield to a hospital by helicopter. There were times when the wounded waited hours and sometimes overnight before they could be airlifted out.

In the first nine months of 1967, 6,990 Americans were killed, a greater number than all those killed in the previous five years. By the end of December 1967, the number of KIA grew to 16,250, roughly forty-four American lives lost per day. It was one of the deadliest years of the Vietnam War.

At that time, it was the longest war in American history, lasting more than ten thousand days with 58,479 Americans dead and at a cost of around $150 billion.

The time spent in combat was unbelievable. During World War II, an infantryman averaged ten days of combat in one year, but in Vietnam, our infantrymen averaged 240 days of combat per year. The saddest part for me was the 58,479 American lives lost. Out of all of those who paid the ultimate sacrifice, it is still hard to understand why God chose to deliver me.

Derl Horn

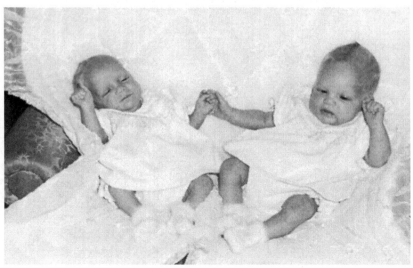

Cathy left and Cindy right one month old

33

HOME WITH FAMILY

After three days at El Toro Air Base, I was discharged and on my way to Arkansas. I called Marilyn to let her know that I would arrive at Drake Air Field the next day. I caught a stand-by flight and arrived in Fayetteville about 11:00 p.m. on February 14, 1968, a cold, snowy Valentine's Day with about six inches of snow on the ground. Our parents were concerned about Marilyn driving with the babies, but she had insisted on meeting me alone with our little family.

As soon as the plane landed and taxied to the gate, I was up and ready to see my sweetheart. I was so anxious to get off the plane that I forgot my carry-on luggage. I had to run back onto the plane to grab it, but I was still the first person off the plane.[31]

I saw Marilyn, my sweet and beautiful wife, running toward me. After many hugs and kisses we walked inside the terminal so I could meet my little daughters, Cindy and Cathy. There they were, still on the couch where Marilyn had left them. They were two and a half months old and the most beautiful babies I had ever seen.

Marilyn: *The day we had dreamed about for months had finally arrived—Derl was coming home on Valentine's Day, February 14, 1968. He was flying into Drake Field in Fayetteville at 11:00 p.m. A few days earlier he had landed at El Toro Marine Corps Air Base where he was discharged from the Marine Corps. I was thrilled and could hardly wait to see him.*

---

[31] At this time you could actually walk into the terminal and out on the tarmac to greet your family.

Blood, Sweat and Honor

Mother had taken a week off from work to care for the babies, allowing us time alone for a short trip together. About mid-day a snow storm moved into the area that turned into a heavy, wet snow, but it didn't dampen my spirits. I was too keyed up with all my preparations for a homecoming party. At lunch mother and dad began to plead with me to leave the babies at home and not take them out with me to the airport, but I would not listen. I was determined that all three of us would be waiting when their daddy stepped off the airplane, so finally they said no more.

That evening I packed my bags and dressed myself and the babies. They looked adorable. Derl's parents arrived and all the family helped bundle the babies and load the car and gave all the usual warnings to be careful. I was a little nervous and apprehensive about the snow, but I was anxious to get to the airport.

We arrived without any problems. I pulled up outside the door of the lobby, unbuckled the first baby and ran her inside, leaving the other one in the car. When I returned for the second baby, there stood my dad holding her in her infant seat. Derl's dad stood in the doorway.

I was shocked. Dad said, "We followed you to make sure you made it okay. We will park the car and let you meet Derl alone." I placed the baby on the couch beside the other baby in front of a large window where I could see the plane as it taxied up to the gate. My heart was pounding, and I could hardly contain myself. It was just moments before the plane stopped and the door on the plane opened. The next few moments were the happiest moments of my life as I saw Derl come bounding down the steps of the plane. I totally forgot I had babies and ran out onto the tarmac to meet him. We hugged and kissed and the world truly stood still. I was thankful that God had brought him back home to me.

Arm in arm, we walked back into the terminal and, to our surprise, a circle of people had gathered around Cindy and Cathy, watching them and smiling at us. It was not hard to see that a reunion was taking place. Derl was in uniform with a dark tan and both of us were in tears with smiles on our faces. Derl walked over to take his first look at his little baby girls. He was speechless. After a few minutes, we picked up the babies, his bags, returned to the car, and headed back home to greet our families.

At home everyone was happy to see Derl and to give him hugs. He was finally able to hold the girls for the first time. We had lots of visiting and laughter, and pictures and movies were taken. Then it was time for us to leave on our trip.

Derl's homecoming had been all we had ever dreamed it would be.

We picked up my sea bag and loaded the babies into the car and drove back to Springdale.³² Arriving back at Marilyn's parent's home, we had a sweet reunion with both sets of parents. I was able to hold my babies for the first time. We took lots of pictures and we talked and talked as we all tried to catch up. Mom Buchanan served dessert and coffee. I was at last safely home with those I loved.

I just couldn't take it all in—those two babies were mine, I was holding my wife, and I was home. We were thrilled to be together.

It was getting late, so we said our good-byes and left for a weeklong second honeymoon, leaving the babies with Marilyn's mom. We spent one glorious night at the Holiday Inn in Fayetteville, about twelve miles from Springdale.

I woke up the next morning, excited about our trip, only to discover it would be short-lived. Marilyn was very sick with a stomach virus. I took her back home, and we called Dr. Edmondson to come by the house to check on her. He told us to be very careful with hygiene and asked that I take care of Marilyn and let her mom take care of the babies. He was concerned about them catching the virus since they were still very small. Coming straight from the battlefield of Vietnam to caring for a sick wife and helping with the newborn babies was a big adjustment for me.

God is good. He has blessed us with many years together, raising our beautiful twin daughters, Cindy and Cathy. Six years later He blessed us with a son, Chris.

In the days ahead, I tried to put Vietnam behind me, but as combat Marines know, this is not possible. I didn't turn to drugs and alcohol to deal with my memories like so many of my war buddies did. I had my faith in God and my loving family to comfort me during the hard times. The war experiences will never go away; they are constantly in my thoughts and dreams.

I know that God delivered me from Vietnam. He had a purpose for my life and that continues to make my life meaningful. I am grateful that with His help I have been blessed with a wonderful, loving family. God bless the United States of America and the United States Marine Corps.

---

³² I did not experience people shouting slurs or spitting on me when I arrived home like many of my Vietnam buddies. Their experiences were sad as they arrived back home to major cities. Many had the humiliation of people yelling and spitting on them, just because they served their country. I felt that I was looked down on because of my Vietnam service, and I didn't feel free to talk about my experience. The media had painted a terrible picture of Vietnam veterans, and many people disagreed and protested the war. Because of this, we did not receive the deserved "Welcome Home" our counterparts in previous wars had received.

CHRISTMAS 1968

Marilyn holding Cindy and Derl holding Cathy

OUR FAMILY

Chris and Jennifer Horn, Peter, Cynthia, Faith and Noah Marshall,
Paisley, Allison, Caspian Cathy and Steve Denton
Derl & Marilyn Horn

THE GRANDCHILDREN
Faith Marshall, Caspian Denton, Derl, Marilyn, Noah Marshall,
Allison and Paisley Denton

EPILOGUE

It was quite an adjustment, leaving the battlefields of Vietnam and five days later arriving home without any transitional or debriefing time. I went from holding a rifle and defending my life to holding my two precious baby girls. I found myself facing a new responsibility to provide for, defend, and protect my new family. I was thrilled to be home in a safe place, but inside there were many conflicting emotions. I wasn't sure how I would learn to manage my emotions when all around me I saw people protesting the war. The processing of all that I had experienced took years and continues even to today. As I look back on my Vietnam days, I still feel blessed to have survived, but I am also sad as I mourn my fallen brothers whose lives were cut short. My desire has been to live my life to honor them and their families who truly gave the ultimate sacrifice.

After Vietnam I continued to deal with the aftermath of combat the result that is now called Post Traumatic Stress Disorder (PTSD). These emotional wounds have caused me to experience daily flashbacks and dreams along with the struggle of "survivor's guilt." I am blessed to have a wonderful, loving, and understanding wife who encourages me to enjoy life, knowing it is a gift from God. My faith and trust in God, who led me during my time in Vietnam and continues to guide me in the recovery process, has made the healing possible. It also helps me to keep my focus on the joy of our twin daughters, our sons-in-law, our son and daughter-in-law, and our five grandchildren. Through the years I have been able to distract myself by being involved in their interests, from church and school activities to sports. I have enjoyed my life much more than most Vietnam veterans.

Within a month after returning home I went to work for an electrical manufacturing company. I tried to forget about Vietnam and all I had experienced. That proved impossible, but I did manage not to mention that I was a veteran due to the anti-Vietnam war feelings at the time. I was able to move quickly into a supervisory position and was later promoted into the Industrial Engineering Department. I retired after 39 years.

I did not discuss the Marines or Vietnam for most of my working career and avoided having contact or attending any Marine Corps functions. In 2006, my brother-in-law Kenneth called to tell me that my Vietnam battalion was having a reunion in Branson, Missouri. He encouraged me to go and offered to go with me. We made it a weekend trip with his wife Karen and Marilyn. It was an emotional reunion after thirty-eight years. I felt the renewed brotherhood. Marilyn and I have attended every reunion of 1st Battalion, 9th Marines, 3rd Marine Division since that time, rekindling old friendships and making many new ones. It has been exciting to make contact with many of the men I served with in Vietnam.

For many years after the Vietnam War, most people did not look favorably upon Vietnam veterans and blamed us for the war instead of recognizing the service we gave for our country. This attitude has changed in the last fifteen years as people have shown their appreciation by shaking my hand and thanking me for my service. It has been a long time coming, but I truly appreciate their gratitude. Many times people offer their appreciation when they see me wearing a Marine Corps or Vietnam cap, or they notice the Purple Heart license plate on our cars. Many servicemen wear these items to show pride in serving our country. I hope we never again see the day when our servicemen and women are not honored and supported for the job they've accomplished for our freedom, along with their families who were left at home

1st Battalion, 9th Marine Regiment, 3rd Marine Division Reunion

MEN WHO FOUGHT IN OPERATION BUFFALO

Gunny Sergeant Leon Burns and Derl Horn

*Ray Linebaugh, Tim Haley, Derl Horn, Steve Weldon, front Richard Huff
At 1/9 3rd Marine Corps Reunion*

The United States Marines Corps Hymn

From the Halls of Montezuma,
To the Shores of Tripoli;
We fight our country's battles
In the air, on land, and sea;
First to fight for right and freedom
And to keep our honor clean;
We are proud to claim the title
Of UNITED STATES MARINES.

Our flag's unfurled to every breeze,
From dawn to setting sun;
We have fought in every clime and place
Where we could take a gun;
In the snow of far off northern lands
And in sunny tropic scenes;
You will find us always on the job --
The UNITED STATES MARINES.

Here's health to you and to our Corps
Which we are proud to serve;
In many a strife we've fought for life
And never lost our nerve;
If the Army and the Navy
Ever look on Heaven's scenes;
They will find the streets are guarded
By UNITED STATES MARINES

Can I ever forget Vietnam?

1. Starving and abused kids and women
2. My Marine buddies who died in combat
3. The open wounds and missing body parts of fellow Marines
4. The fear when the enemy points an AK47 at you with the intent to blow you away
5. The hot piercing pain when mortar shrapnel penetrates your body
6. Being temporarily deaf and the hot piercing pain when a grenade goes off over your head filling your ears with shrapnel
7. The fear and stress of bouncing around on the ground caused from our own bombs from air strikes.
8. The pain and fear of not being able to breathe when napalm is dropped so close it consumes the oxygen in the air.
9. The smell of death from body parts that are days old.
10. The fear of death when you are being bombed for 23 days straight
11. Seeing your dead brothers lying around, mixed with the dead enemy.
12. Loading and stacking dead Marine buddies like sardines onto tanks.
13. Riding with and holding my dead Marine buddies on tanks after removing them from the battlefields.
14. The patrols that expose you daily to snipers and ambushes.
15. Being so dirty that you hate to touch yourself and your raggedy clothes.
16. The ringing in my ears from all the explosions and from firing my Mortar
17. Being caught in an ambush with Mortars, Rockets and grenades falling all around you.
18. Being fired at by small arms fire from the enemy that are hiding in the bush

Can I ever forget Vietnam?

19. Trying to sleep in my foxhole with it full of water.
20. The nonstop rain that wrinkles your skin from head to toe
21. The mud that tries to pull off your boots when you are on the move.
22. Jungle rot from carrying a heavy pack while you are dirty and sweaty and in the rain.
23. The not knowing from day to day whether you or your buddy will be killed
24. Waiting for the next mortar or rocket to hit the hole or bunker that you are in.
25. Being on watch and looking for and seeing the enemy or just a shadow in the night
26. Days on end being subject to sniper fire and incoming mortars and rockets.
27. Falling into a punji pit. (Thank God it was so old that the sharp punji crumbled underfoot.)
28. Discovering that a grenade had come off of my flak jacket and left the pin hanging. (Thank God it was a dud or I would have killed some of my fellow Marines and myself.)
29. Having a helicopter that came in to pick up a wounded Marine land on top of me while I was in my foxhole with my Mortar.
30. Living with mice and rats; trying to sleep while they ran rampant and chewed on my feet.
31. Hearing the whistling sound of a mortar or rocket going past you and fearing that the next one will get you.
32. Waking to the sound of incoming mortars and rockets and utter chaos.
33. Wondering if I will see my wife again or ever see my newborn twin daughters.
34. Being so homesick that you cry.
35. Feeling blamed and betrayed by Americans back home

AUTHOR'S FINAL NOTE

The events that happened in this book are true, recounted from the best of my memory and from the letters Marilyn and I shared with each other during my tour. This is my story and the way I remember it. Others may have seen it from different vantage points and remember it differently, and that is okay. This is how I remember it. Some of the Marines I served with are still alive, but many made the supreme sacrifice for our country.

web page: www.bloodsweatandhonor.ga
email: bloodsweatandhonor@gmail.com

I WILL NEVER FORGET

Made in the USA
Charleston, SC
03 June 2015